F D'Ambrosio

Jan r 84
C B

The Politics of Identity

Ideology and the Human Image

The Politics
of Identity

Ideology and the Human Image

Peter du Preez

BASIL BLACKWELL · OXFORD

© Peter du Preez 1980

First published in 1980 by
Basil Blackwell Publisher
5 Alfred Street
Oxford OX1 4HB
England

All rights reserved. No part of this publication
may be reproduced, stored in a retrieval system,
or transmitted, in any form or by any means,
electronic, mechanical, photocopying, recording
or otherwise, without the prior permission of
Basil Blackwell Publisher Limited.

British Library Cataloguing in Publication Data

Du Preez, Peter
   The Politics of identity.
    1. South Africa — Politics and government —
   20th century
    2. South Africa — Ethnic relations
    3. Ethnicity — Political aspects — Case studies
   I. Title
   301.5'92   JQ1984
   ISBN 0-631-12331-8

Printed in Great Britain by
Billing and Sons Limited
Guildford, London, Oxford, Worcester

Politics was, at first, the art of preventing
people from interfering in matters that
concerned them. To this. in later times,
was added the art of compelling people
to decide matters which they did not
understand.

       Paul Valéry

Contents

Acknowledgements		ix
1	Identity in Politics	1
2	Agents	12
3	Ideology and Identity	43
4	Identity Traps: A Frame and a Con	78
5	Images	111
6	Beyond Ideology	151
References		166
Name Index		173
Subject Index		176

Acknowledgements

Some students owe much to their teachers and some teachers owe much to their students. I count myself among the latter. Peter Collett — who was, many years ago, a student of mine — made so many useful comments on the first draft of this book that it was entirely rewritten.

Then, I wish to record the debt that I owe to colleagues and students of the University of Cape Town. They are tolerant and lively at the same time, happy to put imagination to work and drive out complacency. I cannot easily think of a better place in which to pursue whatever truths one is capable of pursuing.

Jane Hutchings has done wonderful work with untidy manuscript. George Ellis has been kind enough to allow me to reproduce Figure 2 from his Inaugural Lecture.

And my family! Well, what haven't they done?

1
Identity in Politics

> ...not an illustration of appearance as
> a mere sham, but of appearance as a form
> of existence. (Baumann, 1969: 236)

In the following pages, I shall examine one aspect of political activity, its relation to identity. Politics, considered in this aspect, is centrally concerned with maintaining or imposing an identity system. It is concerned with the consolidation of interlocking symbols which give a sense of integrity and continuity to action. A person, like a class or a nation, has a history and a sense of precariously maintained unity. A collective, like a person, can be an agent with an identity relating it to other agents.

Identity cannot be detached from the 'real' interests of agents. One of the consequences of the political consolidation of an identity system is that certain persons are privileged. Firstly, the political agent (nation, state, party or other movements) attempts to win privileges for all or many of its members in relation to the members of other groups. Secondly, within the political entity, there are identities which are more privileged than others. Men may be more privileged than women, adults than children, Protestants than Catholics, citizens than foreigners, whites than blacks,

Brahmins than non-Brahmins — and so forth.

The privileges conferred and the interests served in a political consolidation of identities are often quite clear. It may be that the best jobs, with the highest salaries and most prestige, are reserved for persons of a particular range of identities. This reservation need not be embodied in law. It may even be against the professed intention of the lawmakers. The predominance of persons of a particular identity in positions of power — dispersed throughout society — is often sufficient to maintain an imbalance. And often symbolic force, of which more will be said later, is used to convince the members of excluded classes that they are legitimately excluded. Only occasionally is it necessary to define the excluded identities in explicit law.

It is usually easy enough to see what interests are being served, provided our vision is not too restricted. Society produces a wide variety of goods which satisfy different sorts of people. We should also remember that any transaction in which something is gained — a medal, a citation, an increase in salary, the acclamation of the crowd, a larger carpet for one's office, critical appreciation of one's work, or praise of one's beauty — simultaneously accomplishes several different things. Identity is validated while tangible advantage is obtained. The communal breaking of bread confirms the relation one has to others as well as nourishing the body. The interests of individual persons and groups have often to be discovered in their activities. A religious movement and an army both need money and power, but for the pursuit of different purposes.

When we talk of politics as the consolidation and elaboration of an identity system in which the allocation of opportunities is regulated, we should not apologetically search for the 'material' interests which that system serves, discarding 'aesthetic' and 'spiritual' interests. 'Material' interests are often as little understood (a Buick! a Rolls Royce!) as 'irrational' interests are. Spiritual insight is the reward of some; victory and a slaughtered enemy are the rewards of others. Some wish to grow grain; others hope that their music will be performed. In all these things, men hope for the exchange of symbols of acceptance and admiration while searching for confirmation of what they are; nor do they reject (except in special instances) negotiable symbols which purchase the necessities of both further activity and identity promotion. Harré's (1979) distinction between the expressive and practical aspects of activity, reviving Veblen's (1899) classic recognition of the presentation of self in conspicuous leisure and conspicuous consumption, makes this particularly clear.

Is the choice of *identity* as a central theme in politics an arbitrary one? I believe not. The identity of a group makes political action possible. Subjects and objects of action are constituted by reciprocal appearances and tasks. Without a common identity, individuals cannot form a collective agent. The individual, too, cannot be either the subject or the object of action without an identity which orients him towards others in transactions. Identity is not maintained in isolation. Identities exist in systems of relations — what I shall later call *identity frames* — which maintain each other.

When we examine any system of identities, their reciprocal definition becomes obvious. Masculine identity has its particular meaning in relation to feminine identity; black to white; Protestant to Catholic; proletarian to bourgeois. Context has a marked effect on differentiation as a *process* (Doise, Deschamps and Meyer, 1978).

Relations between identities in a given frame (Marxist, Christian, Liberal) are rendered in accounts of all kinds, from abstract social theory to the folk tales and legends that are told to children. In ceremonies marking the 'birth of the nation' or commemorating a victory, stories which refresh a recognition of our common identity in the heroes of the nation are told. They confirm our collective appearance in the world and give it continuity in time and space.

The first steps in the growth of political movements often takes the form of histories which define a set of relations between the collective and others. The collective may be distinguished from others by a list of grievances and achievements. The positive identity of the collective is affirmed by tales of the early martyrs. Perfectly ordinary people, who were often involved in smuggling and thieving, became heroes. Insignificant events are often taken out of context to model relations between the collective and its opponents.

Josephine Tey gives the Boston Massacre as an amusing example in *The Daughters of Time* (1951). One of the characters in the novel, a young American, says:

Well, I discovered quite by accident, when I was looking up something at College, that the Boston Massacre consisted of a mob throwing stones at a sentry. The total casualties were four. I was brought up on the Boston Massacre, Mr. Grant. (p. 93)

A careful scrutiny of the history of any country will show many incidents of this kind, which have become symbols. These incidents confirm the existence of oppressors and can be used in calls on us to share the identity of the martyrs and to admit the implications of their identity. Once this identification has occurred and has led to reaction, any repressive action simply confirms the relation between the national martyrs and the oppressors. The whole national history is rewritten to confirm this relation and to propound an ideal state of affairs. As Schlegel said: 'Historians are prophets in reverse'. The result is a political movement which attempts to translate symbolic relations into real ones. A South African account of this process can be found in van Jaarsveld (1961).

One of the themes which will run through this book is the tension between persona and person, between man as an identity mobilized in a particular, stylized political role and man as a system of many identities, including political identities, mobilized in many roles. Political ideologies often attempt to animate their agents as personae with finite and mechanical relations to one another. There is, from an ideological point of view, a well understood and predictable relation between collective identity-pairs such as Aryan/Jew; Catholic/Protestant (in Northern Ireland); white/black (in nationalist politics); Basque/Spaniard; or worker/capitalist. Each of these pairs is to be understood in a particular ideology at a particular time and place. Political issues crystallize in such oppositions and ideologies supply us with accounts of them, where an account takes the form of an idealized scenario, including goals, objectives, identities, histories, excuses and justifications. The degree of detail will depend on the amount of work which the intellectuals of the movement have put into the theory. Pamphlets, histories, novels, films, paintings and statues embody the vision.

At first sight it may appear that the concept of *role* can do the theoretical work of *identity*, but that is true at one extreme of a continuum only, when issues have crystallized and men deal with each other as categories in fixed ways. Generally, identity is a broader concept than role, just as person is a broader concept than identity.

The value of this distinction becomes clear when we ask, what is the role of a Basque? of a woman? of a Catholic? In particular identity-pairs, defined within an ideology, the role may be clear. But each of these identities can be engaged in other contrasts, and in episodes beyond the scope of a particular ideology. What happens then is not simple. Each contrast draws on different properties of the identity: a Catholic confronted with the poor, the unconverted, with a friend, engages in different actions. It is only where an identity is defined specifically by one contrast and one episode (or series of episodes conceived as a history), that we can equate identity and role. In general, we may say that:

Roles are identities mobilised in a specific situation; where role is situationally specific, identities are trans-situational. (Scott and Lyman, 1972: 424)

Locutions such as 'the role of a woman', or 'the role of a Basque' are usually attempts to pre-empt the implications of womanhood or 'Basqueness' for a particular purpose. They are, when they are not specific, attempts to absorb categories of persons to particular roles; to make these roles of such importance that anyone of the designated category who fails to perform them can be made to feel guilty or ashamed.

Questions such as: 'Is that the way a woman (or Basque) behaves?' are *identity traps*, which are devices of great social significance. The consequence of such an attribution is that the person has to justify or excuse his behaviour within the attributed identity frame. It is assumed that the behaviour of a woman or a Basque — to continue using our example — is well understood as a system of implications of the category. Usually, this means defining a situation (or even an extended scenario) in which the person is predictable.

The distinction between *person* and *identity* should also be made clear. The value of this distinction is seen when we examine the possible identities of a single person who is a Catholic, a woman, a Basque, a worker and a cripple. Each of these identities can be mobilized (perhaps jointly) in several episodes. Identity is appearance-for-self-and-others; person is a system of identities.

Identities are not equal. A person may feel that he has a 'real' identity, a central self from which he speaks most truthfully. The core identity must be created out of the relation between the appearances of his self, so that he may speak as himself — as Tolstoy or Freud — and not as one of his parts.

This is the 'style of one's individuality', the 'awareness of self-sameness and continuity' that was absent in Erikson's patients suffering a loss of identity (Erikson, 1968: 50). Erikson cites both William James and Freud on the experience

of a 'real self' among their other selves:
> James: '... a voice inside which speaks and says: "This is the real self!"' (p. 19)
>
> Freud, on his Jewishness: '...a clear consciousness of inner identity, the safe privacy of a common mental construction'. (p. 22)

A coherent style, sense of integrity and continuity, do not depend on the abolition of our different identities. That would be reverting to personae. What is required is that identities be coordinated as the words of a language are coordinated in the expression of a particular message. The system of identities is a social 'tool box' (Devereux, 1975), just as the vocabulary of a language is, but persons have the task of saying something, of generating from their vocabulary an 'identity-sentence' of a particular style and purpose.

The distinction between identity and person is also clear when we ask this question: 'Can I hold an identity responsible for an act?' The answer is, I think, quite clear. We hold a person responsible. He cannot say: 'As a Basque I am guilty but as the father of family I am innocent.'

A term which is often used more or less interchangeably with identity is *self*, and for this reason the relation between self and identity ought to be made clear. Identity is the appearance of self; it is the way self is perceived and understood by persons. Self is a component of the psychological processes by which we explain behaviour, and identity is the appearance of self in that process. Self is, therefore, an 'inductive generalization from behavioural data' (Devereux, 1975: 52), while identity is exhibited in the form of monitored performances. Identity is the performance of a self in the total system of a personality engaged in an episode. Erikson's account of the relation between ego and identity may be helpful in grasping the relation between self and identity posited here.

The ego is unconscious, an organizing system of the personality: 'we become aware of its work, but never of it' (Erikson, 1968: 218). The unconscious work of the ego results in 'images and personified Gestalten' (p. 59). The success of the work of the ego is discovered in an awareness of ego identity ('style of one's individuality' (p. 50)) and personal identity ('selfsameness and continuity' (p. 50)).

A self-system is known by its work; its action is unconscious. Persons have a number of self-systems (Mair, 1977; Shaw and McKnight, 1979; McKellar, 1977; Osgood, Luria, Jeans and Smith, 1976) which the ego attempts, more or less successfully, to reconcile by discovering 'style' and 'continuity'.

This synthesis is not always successful and when it fails there is a loss of identity and a fragmentation of the personality.

The fragmentation of persons is a political problem and by that I do not mean a problem for politicians. In political movements, we are mobilized as collective agents with a common identity. There are differences in the degree to which events are structured so as to reduce us to that identity: fragmentation of roles, terror, information control, distance from our victims, anonymity, indoctrination and other factors may contribute to such a reduction. Though these must surely count as mitigating factors in attributing responsibility — to the extent that a man falls into a particular identity trap he is no longer a responsible person — this introduces a moral obligation to resist such a reduction.

The architecture of this book will be provided by C. W. Mill's (1963) conception of the obligations of political philosophy. Though this is not a political philosophy, the same sort of problems must be touched on in a less ambitious way.

Mills proposes that a political philosophy should contain a statement of ideals, a discussion of agencies, an ideology and a theory.

Let me turn to the first.

A work in politics should state the values in which it is rooted. In this book what I shall say about political values will be contained in one paragraph. I take it as a fundamental premise that men should resist any reduction to personae. This implies a rejection of pre-emptive construing (Kelly, 1955) and an obligation to diminish the sphere of influence of all 'imperatively coordinated systems' (Dahrendorf, 1959), whether they be schools, armies, business corporations or states. The power of large, imperatively coordinated institutions means that our 'public' identity becomes predominant and our 'private' identity is weakened. We see ourselves as patients rather than agents, our behaviour as caused rather than chosen, and our lives as belonging to others rather than to ourselves (Baumann, 1969). The present tendency all over the world to create larger states, more centralized education, and more centralized transport, monetary and welfare systems, under the control of a larger and larger bureaucracy, seems to me pernicious and unnecessary. In other words, I support the goals of Illich (1973): restore choice to the individual and conviviality to human relations. Even the most personal human activities, such as learning, have been bureaucratized as 'schooling'. Our learning is not personal or chosen, it is done to us. Minor reforms in education cannot change this. This is not the place to attempt to show how we may limit centralized power by creating cross-cutting and competing organizations, but my values are relevant to an understanding of one of the themes of the book, a tension between person and persona, between the individual as an orchestrator and composer of identities and the individual as a standardized performer of roles. This tension is not simply a function of intra-individual psychology; it is a function of the way in which the individual is acted or lived by institutions. To restore their lives to individuals it is necessary to allocate resources over which they can dispose in determining their own learning, their own spending and working. At the moment, vast bureaucracies spend their money for them on education and welfare. Hayek (1978) has argued the case for more restrictions on legislators. I am arguing that it is essential to reduce the division between public and private identity, not by increasing the public sphere, as is the case in the drearier varieties of socialism, but by socializing the private. This means creating the conditions of liberty and choice for individuals. To use John Stuart Mill's distinction: the social constitution of liberty will make the achievement of individual freedom possible.

What I have said here may be taken simply as an attitude. It is not fully argued and will not be in this book. Nevertheless, it is an attitude which will colour much of what I say. The bulk of the book will be concerned with agencies and ideology.

The second requirement of a political philosophy is that it must say something about the agencies which will bring about and maintain the state of affairs which is desired. In this book, discussion of agencies will be limited to a discussion of the identity of individual and collective agents. No suggestions concerning strategy, recruitment or organization will be attempted. I shall focus strictly on the question: how does identity enter the activities of political agents?

The third requirement of a political philosophy is that it should provide an ideology. Since this is a work on political psychology, I shall attempt to show how ideologies function in providing accounts of the relation between identities. Not all political ideologies are equal. It follows from my statement of values that I prefer those ideologies which promote Illich-type decentralization. Such ideologies make space for the person: they do not take the form of deadly utopias, such as Plato's *Republic*. Nor do they continually justify or excuse action by consulting a sacred political text, the way Maoist or Marxist-Leninist communists do. An important question may be posed. What limits does ideology place on choice of action and thought? Are we to conceive of an ideology as a determinate and self-contained system, beyond which we cannot think? Does collective solipsism replace individual solipsism? If this is the case, how can we ever compare ideologies? This is the problem of *incommensurability* that has loomed so large in the discussion of Kuhn-type paradigms of scientific knowledge, but it is worth extending the discussion to look at ideologies in the same way.

Finally, a political philosophy should state a theory of society. Here, a much more limited question will be asked. What is the relation between persons and ideologies? What are the properties of agents who can question their own identity and its place in the ruling ideology of the day?

2
Agents

INDIVIDUAL AND COLLECTIVE AGENTS

Politics is — among other things — a dispute about who gets what under which circumstances. Sometimes the dispute focuses on 'objective' circumstances, but it can easily be shown that the implications of a situation or an issue can only be understood when the framework of identities is known (see Chapter 5). Politics is as much facework as spadework, to rephrase Harré's (1979) distinction between the expressive and practical aspects of social activity.

The dispute of politics is conducted by agents, both collective and individual. It is important to grasp at all times that individual persons may be *both* individual agents and members of a collective agent in a particular action. Because we can identify a person individually and describe his individual actions, this does not mean that he is not, at the same time, participating in a collective action. An army on the move is a collective agent; yet we can describe the movements of each individual in that army. Describing the action of a collective agent (the Eighth Army engaged the Afrika Korps at 5 a.m.) does not mean that we cannot, at the same time, describe what Corporal Fred Jones did.

Often, it is a matter of choice which we decide to look at.

We may wish to describe the actions of a collective rather than an individual person for the sorts of reasons that an astronomer wishes to describe a galaxy rather than an individual star. The collective, like the galaxy, has properties which differ from those of the individual. Often, we can understand the individual only if we understand the collective. This is true of galaxies and collective agents for rather different reasons.

The important thing to grasp about a collective agent is that it is composed of individuals who are attempting to work out a common appearance for others and for themselves. Each one in the collective has some myth about what the collective is and how it appears to certain others. This is the identity of the collective. It consists of a name and many more or less coordinated descriptions, which are often called stereotypes. These descriptions are not merely characterizations (stubborn, rich, pleasure-loving); they are also categorizations (born in France; educated Lycée Condorcet; lives in Paris). Collective identity is as difficult to describe as individual identity for a very good reason. It emerges in context. 'Who are you?' makes little sense until we know the context of the question: in relation to whom? doing what? when? Then, out of the resources of shared history, the appearance is fashioned.

For obvious reasons, politicians spend much time defining the identities of collectives they hope to move (with themselves in the lead!). The powerful image which crystallizes identity in a particular action is the tool of the statesman of genius.

What do collective and individual agents have in common?
1 Both have an identity – a name, an appearance, and a history.
2 The appearance of an agent can be monitored and presented to others. That is, the agents we are discussing are also actors. Much work is done by pamphleteers, PR men and politicians in getting the appearance right.

3 Agents have a subjective form, an inner community, the nature of which is defined in particular relations with others. Corresponding to this subjective form is the use of the first person, 'I' or 'we'.
4 Agents can take roles. A regiment can be assigned a particular role in a battle, for example.
5 Agents can be praised, blamed, or other moral descriptions can be attributed to them. Since individuals act *both* as individuals and as members of a collective they may be blamed while the collective is praised or vice versa. Or they may simply share whatever praise or blame is given to the collective as a whole.
6 Agents initiate performances. We may chose to end an account of an action by referring to properties of the agent. However, we may wish to go further and give an account of how the agent is constituted (how does a person come to want X? how does a school come to have a particular tradition?).

Having outlined some of the properties of both collective and individual agents, I shall now discuss some of these in greater detail.

First, there is the question of the subjective form of the agent.

Roman Jakobson (1963) refers to the first person pronoun as a 'shifter' — a grammatical entity that can only be defined in relation to a message. The person-who-speaks is an 'I', from his own perspective. And 'I' is always in contrast to 'you' — it is not one of the primitive experiences of childhood, which is why it is such a troublesome pronoun for children. Now, what happens when 'I' becomes the plural 'we'? The result is what Benveniste (1966) calls a 'false plural', a conjunction of 'I' and 'not-I'. Yet all plurals are false plurals, since there are no identical events in the universe. 'We' is a collection of events that are, like all other events, similar in certain respects and different in other respects. It is an experience of subjectivity in individuals who share a position in relation to the position of others — and that position is an identity. When a subject experiences himself as part of a collective agent, he is not adding 'I' and 'not-I', but postulating a common subjectivity for all the individuals making up that agent.

It is an error to suppose that 'I' is a constant. It is not. It is a relation. To the extent that it is identically determined in different individuals by a common relation, it is a true plural, a 'we'. This is no attempt to discover a 'group mind' — it is an attempt to discover the conditions under which 'I' subjectivity becomes 'we' subjectivity in individual agents. To use an analogy, we are examining the same atom when its electrons have jumped orbit. The 'I' subjectivity becomes a 'we' subjectivity in individuals who share a common construction of their relation to others. It is their change of subjective state that makes collective agents possible.

Besides the use of the first person, what do we expect of any agent? We expect that it can perform actions, that it can engage in an act-action structure of the sort described by Harré and Secord (1972) where an act is a performance that has meaning. Now, some acts can only be performed by individuals forming a collective agent: playing rugby or any team sport is an example. The accounts of the act refer to the team as well as to the performance of individuals. It is the whole team which opposes another whole team, not simply Cliff Morgan who opposes some other individual. There is nothing mysterious in this. We merely say that certain kinds of acts cannot be performed by individuals. They must form a team, a collective agent of some kind, with an organization of its own, to make the act possible. We can see both the team and the individual; we can refer to the acts of the individual as they form part of the act of the team as a whole.

Another feature of any agent is that it must take

responsibility for its actions. An individual must take responsibility — that is part of our conception of a person performing an action. If he commits a crime, the fact that he was playing a part, or that he was role-playing, or following orders, does not absolve him of all responsibility. These might, under certain circumstances, mitigate his responsibility, but the responsibility would be his. If he did not accept responsibility for any of his actions, we could not regard him as a person. Even an actor in a play, following a script, is responsible for his performance of a role. He is not responsible for the things his character does, but for the way he represents him as doing his things. His act is to render that action for the audience.

This is true of collective agents as well. We hold a team responsible for its bad performance or its victory. This in no way denies that we can blame or praise individuals for the way their actions contributed to the total act of the team. There is no either/or in this. Those who are familiar with work on language will know that an utterance may count as several acts (Austin, 1962).

In the same way, a team performance may be viewed as the acts of individuals and as the acts of a collective. The result of the match is the responsibility of individuals *and* the team, with its cohesiveness, its playing together, its style, to which all the individuals contribute.

The individual cannot replace the team, nor the team the individual.

What else do we expect of an agent? We expect it to have continuity, to have an identity which is not reducible to that of its parts, to have a name and a reputation.

This is true of both individual and collective agents.

We can't (as a rule) say that Jones *is* the team. The team has its own name. Nor is the reputation of the team Jones's reputation, or the history of the team Jones's history.

A distinction is commonly made between 'personal' and 'social' identity. The first is maintained by unique 'identity pegs' — the unique history of the individual, the differences which he elaborates in creating his own distinctive approach to others. The second refers to what is common to actors of the same category — 'in what sense do those who know some know many' (Goffman, 1968: 82). One might at first suppose that here we have the break between individual and collective agents, but very little reflection will show that this is not so. If we change the terms to ones that are more appropriate, we see that this same contrast applies to collective agents. What Goffman is drawing attention to, in using the terms 'personal' and 'social', is 'distinctive' and 'common' features of identity. These are quite clearly to be found in collective agencies. The regiment, the team, the political party, must build up distinctive 'identity pegs' in addition to those they have in common with all other regiments, teams and political parties. It is in the elaboration of distinctive elements of identity that the group enables the individual to achieve the richest subjective construal of himself, both as an individual in contrast with other individuals, and as a team member contrasting with other team members. The individual uses what Tajfel (1978) calls his 'social identity' in both group/group and individual/group contrasts.

In structuring group/group contrasts, the subjective richness of the experience will depend on the reputation, history and tradition of the group. This is the pool on which all members of the collective draw in achieving a consensus about what it means to be a member.

DIFFERENTIATION OF AGENTS

The rise of new agents is as important in the life of politics as the consolidation of old ones. A new class is mobilized, and the support for an existing form of government is destroyed; or an existing nationalist movement, stimulated by foreign intervention, strengthens an already powerful regime.

What I wish to attempt is a sketch for a theory of the evolution of identity in both collective and individual agents. Since agents attempt to gain various social goods, and since they vary in the degree of their success, we can see how a theory might begin. What is the minimum number of assumptions we have to make — recognizing that such assumption depends on a further network of assumptions, all complex?

One has to plant one's flag somewhere, to begin one's argument as best one may.

It is both sensible and convenient to draw heavily on the body of theory and experiment created by Tajfel and his colleagues in their 1978 volume, *Differentiation between Social Groups*. Any theorist in this area must be grateful for the many leads provided there. Much of what I have to say will be influenced by various contributors to the volume, though much will be different.

Tajfel begins with the assumption that individuals compare and evaluate the groups to which they belong, striving for positive evaluation of their own group — and of themselves, as members of that group. Moscovici and Paichler, in the same volume, add a general proposition: majorities sure of their position and success — what they call 'nomic' majorities — can afford to be generous to minorities, perhaps not to the extent of evaluating the minority more positively than they do the majority, but to the extent of being fair, of admitting some minority virtues and some majority faults. This depends upon an unassailable confidence, upon a superiority that can afford to be generous.

My own starting point will be slightly different from Tajfel's, and closer to that of Lemaine, Kastersztein and Personnaz (1978). In the social world, there has always been room for a range of different agents, each with a particular world view, each occupying a special niche in the human ecology. Some of these are in direct competition, others exploit different resources. Their forms of life are often incommensurable: it is no use trying to judge them all by their success in producing refrigerators. The production of imaginary worlds has always been the major human activity, since it is in these that activity has meaning and identity is defined. But even there, in the creation of imaginary worlds, the competition is intense (as the intolerance of rival art movements and religions demonstrates!).

I shall state these assumptions and their implications in the following pages. Many human psychological properties must, of necessity, be taken for granted in stating these assumptions and drawing their implications. One takes it for granted that individuals can perceive, recognize, think, draw comparisons, recognize their own needs, and do many more things. Each assumption is grounded on further assumptions. 'To be sure, there is justification, but justification comes to an end.'

After stating my assumptions, I shall discuss each one separately and then proceed to draw some implications which are of importance to the life of politics. Many more implications could be drawn from these assumptions, for different purposes.

Assumptions

Interaction: Agents monitor the identities they negotiate in social interaction.

Competition: Agents are selected by their success in competing for scarce resources.

Open and closed ideologies: Societies differ in the extent to which the dominant ideology is open or closed. Open ideologies show the world as a plurality of possible social systems and categories of persons; closed ideologies show the world as a single valid social system and set of categories of persons.

THE INTERACTION ASSUMPTION

Why is it necessary to monitor our identity and the identities of those we are relating to? Obviously, it would be difficult to commit murder, mayhem or marriage without some idea of who we are and who the other parties are. That, it may be said, requires very little monitoring. But I want, in addition, to know how I'm doing as a particular identity. Am I credible as a lover? Do I issue commands with conviction? What does the other person think of my performance and what do I think of his? Is *he* issuing commands with conviction? Can he be discredited and embarrassed in the 'presentation of self' (Goffman, 1969)? Many actions — perhaps all actions — require that identity be properly established for the act to be successful. To accept someone's promise means that one has to accept him as a sincere person. The art of identifying fascinates us to such an extent that much of our dramatic art and fiction is devoted to establishing identity (and hence an account). An actor who performs well on the stage succeeds in establishing an identity for us and in so doing he establishes the 'meaning' and 'significance' of the events we have seen. Negotiating and monitoring identity in social interaction are both necessary. The other does not necessarily accept my presentation of myself, does not necessarily wish to be the person I make him become in my presentation of myself. If I am a reliable borrower, is he a generous creditor? If I am a lover, is she? If I am a father, is this young man a son? Each of these relationships must be negotiated and the performance monitored to see whether identity has been properly established.

A paradoxical case appears to arise when the self is presented as no one, which is what Robbe-Grillet proposes for his characters and Solange Marriot carries to extremes in *Nothing, or the Consequence*. Robbe-Grillet tells us that the novel of character belongs to the past, to the age of individualism (1963: 28). The writer has nothing to say, merely a manner of saying it. This manner of saying invents a relation to the world – that of evasion. Yet, 'The writer...can only enter into his quiet negotiations with the reader; he urges the reader kindly to assume...to believe...to accept as good coin...(Lem, 1979: 4). What happens if nothing happens, if 'the train did not arrive' and 'he did not come'?

What we are recording is the vanishing of a significant other with whom to negotiate, from whom to live at a carefully judged distance in the appearance one presents. Appearance, in this symbolic world, has vanished. What one is left with is 'the burning, not what burns'. As Bertrand Russell says of modern physics, 'what burns' has disappeared. Matter is no longer solid. It has become Heraclitean Fire (1961: 65).

Here we have a demonstration of the fact that subjective reality and identity exist as a relation. The vanishing of Gods and the decay of humanism reduce man to a mechanism – a series of events without identity – a perception, a memory, a possibility for which no one can take responsibility. The Gods are waiting, whether they belong to this world or another, to awaken a reluctant opposition, making action mysterious and significant, intelligible and paradoxical.

THE COMPETITION ASSUMPTION

Social agents compete for recognition, acclaim, social position, material necessities and all the other goods of different ways of life. If individuals do not obtain the necessities of life, they die and collective agents die with them. If they do not receive recognition, they change, oppose, or sink into despair.

Under what social conditions do groups become competitive? And under what social conditions do members of a group identify strongly with that group?

The work of Tajfel (1978) and Turner (1975) shows us that the mere existence of another group in a laboratory test will induce competitive behaviour, even when the groups are *not* negatively interdependent; that is, the rewards due to a group do not depend on its performing better than the other group. If this is the case, what are the groups competing for? Turner proposes that 'groups aim to move to more positive value in comparison with other groups' (1975: 26).

What does the individual get out of a group? According to Tajfel (1972) he derives from it a 'place in society' and a positive identity (p. 293) which can only be assured if his group can be positively evaluated in relation to other groups. Hence the competition. Hence, also, the preservation of the distinctiveness of groups which are particularly successful at conferring the benefit of a positively evaluated identity on their members. Since all of us belong to many possible groups, we have to determine in each comparison what group membership is being used. This is rarely difficult. The supporters of different football teams may all be Methodists, but for the purpose of the current conflict they are members of rival groups, seeking enhancement, each through the victory of his own team.

Some of the conditions of social competition and strong group identity are listed by Turner (1975). Categorization must be clear; the dimensions of comparison must be recognized by both groups; actions must be similarly evaluated by both groups; and there must be some possibility of a change in comparative evaluation (p. 22).

What are the responses of individuals to inferior group membership? They may attempt to leave the group — and the phenomenon of 'passing' is known in all societies where people conceal their religious affiliations, their race, their working-class origins, their caste or their family. They may attempt to change the dimension of comparison and achieve a special niche in society (spiritual values are substituted for material; intellectual for economic); they may attempt a transvaluation of characteristics (blackness, femaleness, jewishness, or whatever) by aggressive action; or they may sink into despair and adopt the qualities of the 'good' servant (Vaughan, 1978, discusses some of these).

It is impossible to eliminate competition between groups, if this theory is correct. Nor would it be desirable, since individuals derive positive identity from group membership. What can be done is to attempt to regulate some of the forms which group competition takes. Under some conditions, it appears to be possible to prevent the competition from becoming too destructive. One such way is to attempt to create cross-cutting divisions and thus prevent a particular division from absorbing all others in the political arena (Dahrendorf, 1959). The extreme difficulty of achieving such a fracturing of major groupings is seen in Cyprus, Northern Ireland, South Africa, Zimbabwe, Israel or wherever particular identities are repeatedly mobilized in conflicts. These then determine the major groupings in the search for political power and parties which seek to transcend these groupings find that they have no power base.

It is these group structures that provide the agencies of political action. In the desperate discussions of politics common among liberals in deeply divided societies, there is very little reference to the agencies that will bring about a desired state of society. How can violently hostile groups be persuaded not to be violently hostile? How can mutually reinforcing divisions be eliminated? How can different group identities be mobilized in discussing the political problems that till now have been reduced to simple oppositions of two poles?

Politically active members of groups often promote group distinctiveness in order to gain power. Their emphasis on group characteristics eliminates competition from outside in their quest for control of the group itself, and as pioneers of the view that the group has its own identity they establish their claim to lead it. In the larger areas of society they then have a basis for an assault on the citadels of power.

Here I have referred to men who promote existing

characteristics. Even more radical are the claims of those who create movements, whether in science, religion or politics (Freud, Marx, Lenin, Luther, Christ, Mohammed).

It has already been pointed out that groups compete even if they are not negatively interdependent, even if there is no limited cake which they have to share. Naturally, to the extent that resources are limited, competition intensifies. Tajfel and his colleagues have focused on material rewards (coins which are distributed) in their rejection of the view that groups have to be negatively interdependent to compete, yet a little reflection will show that groups are always negatively interdependent − they cannot all win the same acclaim, prestige or status. There is always a shortage of pre-eminence. By focusing on the monetary rewards which are distributed, this is neglected, in spite of the fact that, to relatively affluent students, winning is more important than obtaining a small sum of money.

Various identity markers, such as wage differentials, may be maintained to preserve what are thought to be proper distinctions between groups of people (e.g., Brown, 1978). A complication in industry is that the cake is usually limited, so that differentials serve both the function of marking distinctions and the function of gaining a larger share for privileged groups relative to others.

An example of the interplay of the preservation of distinctions and of negatively interdependent rewards is seen in the South African gold mines, where for over half a century the ratio of black to white wages has been stable at about 1:10. In 1911 the ratio was 1:9; in 1931 the ratio was 1:10.6, and in 1961 the ratio was 1:14.2 (Wilson, 1972).

Johnstone (1976) contrasts two hypotheses about racial domination in the South African mining industry. The first is that racial domination is dysfunctional and an irrational consequence of prejudice. This would be the equivalent of an hypothesis that differences are maintained purely as a function of social competition between groups. The second hypothesis is that racial domination has been economically advantageous to both employers and white employees wishing to preserve a relatively favoured position and a larger slice of the cake for themselves. The first hypothesis is questionable (as a complete explanation) because it cannot explain the extensive involvement of property-owners in the system of racial domination. Johnstone also argues, less cogently (and emphasizing the term 'irrational'), that the first hypothesis cannot explain the enormous economic expansion that has taken place in spite of racial domination, nor its persistence in the face of economic growth.

The argument is not conclusive. From the employers' point of view, wages may be divided in any way that does not prevent recruitment. If inequitable division leads to fewer labour difficulties, they will accept such a division. It may even accord with their own 'irrational' assumptions about the relative status of black and white. A much more convincing argument, drawing on our experience of the tenacity with which differentials are maintained in every industrial system, is that the exploitation of black workers on the gold mines serves *both* the group identity of whites ('irrational') *and* the economic interests of white workers (larger slice of the cake) and employers (lower wage bill).

OPEN AND CLOSED IDEOLOGIES

Some ideologies encourage social experiment; others already embody the perfect society and will permit little change (Popper, 1966).

An ideology is not simply a collection of ideas. It is akin to the concept of 'paradigm' advanced by Kuhn, or 'language game' as found in Wittgenstein. In neither case is there a clear definition. What we can do is point to a number of features which are more or less present in ideologies, paradigms and language games, without taking on too much of the burden that must be carried in the next chapter. Included in the concept of paradigm are 'universally recognized scientific achievements that for a time provide model problems and solutions to a community of practitioners' (Kuhn, 1962: x), and also the unanalysed, accepted aspects of scientific practice, including 'laws, theory, application, and instrumentation together' (p. 10). 'Science can be seen as a fully human activity, governed by rules, conventions and grammar – like any other human activity. Science is a game in which the rules are changed as we go along' (Phillips, 1977: 65).

What is important is that problems are solved within a paradigm, with a particular set of intellectual tools, institutions and instruments.

It is also worth looking at the concept of a language game. There are all kinds of language games, such as specific technical languages, everyday language games, and language games which use arithmetic, mathematics and physical events linked in particular ways. The concept of 'paradigm' requires us to assume that one language game – or a small set of linked language games – comes to be the accepted means of solving certain problems. These language games are activities in which world-views are maintained in giving orders, thanking people, measuring grain in exchange for money, or foxhunting. The important thing is that nature is not out there waiting to be viewed as a significant pattern: meaning is something we have to make. This is something to bear in mind when considering the cruder ideologies of materialism and economic determinism.

A language game – and, for that matter, a paradigm – is not arbitrary. Language games are conducted in the context of the 'natural history' of our species (Wittgenstein, 1953: 467). Human thinking, language and agreement in judgements (such as the unpleasantness of pain) are all part of our 'natural history.

Given these facts of 'natural history', though, the games

are human inventions.

When we examine human ideologies (Christianity, Islam, Marxism), we see that they have the same family of characteristics as paradigms and language games. They are, in fact, paradigmatic language games for constructing a view of the world in which our lives have significance. They are not arbitrary. They must take cognizance of 'social facts' and of our 'natural history', but, that granted, they are incalculably variable.

Here, I do not propose to go fully into the question of the nature of ideology. What I do wish to say is that ideologies solve certain critical human questions (who are the elect? what is the meaning of happiness? and suffering? what should we do to be saved? what kind of society is just?) and contain conventions, rules, theory, epistemological assumptions, and practices. How does one attain truth? By fasting? Meditating? Experimenting? Killing off the opposition? A collection of approved texts, myths recited over television (during the 'news') and methods of education, are examples of the ideological apparatus of the state.

What I do wish to assert is that some ideologies are more tentative and experimental than others. Some rely on a few fundamental assumptions and improvise the rest; others rely on the dogmatic interpretation by a central authority of a sacred text.

To take distant and relatively uncontroversial examples of open and closed ideologies, we may contrast the Athens of the fifth century BC and Sparta in the seventh. Devereux (1975) remarks of the Spartans that their sayings are ritualistic and typical, and of the Athenians that they were typical only in being so very different from one another. Spartan institutions and practices were intended to maintain a fixed order, those of Athens to promote individualism (Gerth and Mills, 1954).

The most important features of what I called closed ideologies is that they do these three things:

(a) The range of identities (social categories) is relatively fixed and the relations between them prescribed; and
(b) individuals are largely categorized at birth; it is held that their categorization is inherent; and
(c) there is a relatively fixed interpretation of the nature of society and politics.

Caste societies, totalitarian societies, societies with an aristocratic order based on birth, and racist societies are examples of societies in which ideology is closed, though in different ways.

It cannot be contended that some ideologies are open in all respects and others are closed in all respects, but that they can be placed (approximately) on a continuum from closed to open, using the criteria above.

There is another dimension of ideology, namely *richness*, which would be worth exploring. A rich ideology is one which has many resources — a complex and supple syntax of relations and a large number of categories. An illustration from music may make it clear how such an ideology might make social invention possible. When we compare the innovation which is possible within the monodic frame, following a single line, and that which polyphony (introduced in the tenth century) makes possible, we see that the latter is a richer theory and leads to more variety.

Similarly, when we compare Sparta and Athens, we are impressed not only by the different in openness and closedness but even more by the differences in richness.

Implications

Of the many possible implications of the assumptions stated above, I shall attempt to draw out only a few which are important to the themes of this book.

All implications will be briefly stated and then separately discussed.

The first implication is that men may be manoeuvred into *identity traps*; that is, positions in which they cannot disown a particular identity which is attributed to them. This is a consequence of the fact that identity is negotiated, but not freely. Identity is negotiated within the assumptions of an ideology, taking the immediately applicable form of an identity frame.

The second implication of the fact that identity is negotiated (and monitored) is that it is *problematic*. What moves should I make? What identity should I attempt to achieve in particular contexts? And even, what contexts should I choose, where I can choose, for my actions? Again, what has been said about ideology is important in determining ranges of choice and contexts. We all have a questionable relation to our own identity, as it is presented in particular events. This is not a 'private' matter. Some of the most crucial questions of our time have been political — our relation to authority and what it demands of us.

The third implication is that there is a greater *pressure to change* when there is a greater competition for scarce resources. But this pressure is not a mechanical one. It depends upon the orchestration of self that is possible within given ideological contexts, and on the relation which a person has to the appearances he presents. In other words, the pressures that lead to change arise both in the outside world (how can I get what I want?) and in internal dissatisfactions and aspirations (how can I become what I want to be?).

The fourth implication is that some changes will lead to *revolution* and others to consolidation or *evolution* of social structures. If movement from one collective to another is relatively free, for qualified persons, then a given social structure is likely to be maintained (though evolutionary changes occur). If movement of persons is not possible for ideological reasons, then any change which occurs must be revolutionary. This is not so much an explanation of evolution and revolution as a description of the kind of change likely to occur under open and closed ideologies. It simply draws out the meaning of open and closed ideology, in a tautology.

Now I shall examine each of these implications rather more fully.

IDENTITY TRAPS

Agents who share an assumption about the range of identities and the relations between them in a particular society share an identity frame. More will be said about this in Chapters 3 and 4. An agent who succeeds in imposing an identity frame on another has got the other in an identity trap. Usually, this manoeuvre is to the advantage of the agent who imposes the frame, but not all advantages are obvious or rational, in an economic sense.

In politics, the advantages are usually clear: they are material and existential. Others are manoeuvred into identity traps in order to confirm one's superiority, or one's view of the world, or to add to one's wealth.

Control is an important feature of most negotiations. A colonel barking out his commands may succeed in controlling the identity of a man who was his subordinate, though they have both left the army. A teacher in a classroom may manipulate signals in such a way that he convinces his pupils of his right to define the learning task. Skill as well as brute force enter negotiations of this kind. In fact, the tools used in defining situations must act on the assumptions and immediate responses of the negotiators to be completely successful.

Such devices as 'double bind' (Bateson *et al.*, 1956) and 'paradoxical communication' (Watzlawick *et al.*, 1968) are manoeuvres which may be more or less deliberately undertaken. Berne (1967) has described a large number of 'games' which, from the present perspective, manoeuvre people into identity traps. Much political work is expended on identity traps. An example in South Africa is the creation of ethnic homelands which support the identity frame of the government — but many examples could be drawn from the daily political practice of every government in the world. The current insistence by many leaders that there are no politically relevant ethnic differences in South Africa is equally an identity trap, playing on universalistic assumptions.

To create a completely successful identity trap all parties should be manoeuvred into sharing the same identity frame. It should come to seem inevitable, natural and indisputable. If the division is between black and white, between one ethnic group and another, or between Islam and Christianity, when all parties see the division in those terms, the trap is sprung.

Since we always adopt one frame or another, these frames have to be *evaluated*. This is a problem which is discussed in Chapter 4.

IDENTITY IS PROBLEMATIC

We sometimes talk as though identity were a mask to be put on, as though it were something 'found' in an already finished state. This is not the case. Each person has to make something of the identity elements he finds in his community. He has, to use an analogy, to speak his own 'identity-sentences'.

The proper presentation of an identity is a skilled performance, as Goffman has pointed out. It is in this performance that we can find the germs of change. We stand at a distance from it, we exercise skill in bringing it off with some degree of conviction and plausibility, we search for authenticity and a style of our own.

> Each mortal thing does one thing and the same:
> Deals out that being indoors each one dwells;
> Selves — goes itself; *myself* it speaks and spells,
> Crying *Whát I dó is me: for that I came.*
> (Gerard Manley Hopkins: As kingfishers catch fire)

We find the consequences of this attempt to discover that personal note in even the most casual negotiations.

Consider an example in which a man comes home late, perhaps a little drunk:

> 'Is that the way for a husband to behave?'
> 'I'm a man.'
> 'You're the father of two children.'
> 'I'm a man, I tell you. A man!'

In this event, the man insists on an identity that would leave him free of the roles his wife attempts to impose. The implication is that he is free to do as he chooses.

The meanings of various identity relations are discovered in such accounts, as Scott and Lyman (1972) point out.

Certain agents exist for the performance of particular acts. In fact, their identity may be said to be constituted in their proper performance of these acts. A regiment which does not fight (when required), a rugby club which exists solely to enable its members to drink together, or a school in which no learning is attempted, seem to be failing in their core roles.

Identity is never simply given, even when we appear to be 'found' by it in an ideological system, or a *discours transindividuel* (Lacan, 1966). It is true that we have the elements of an identity, presented as a name, a history, a social class, a family reputation, attributions, and so forth. But these elements are like the forms of our language. Language is all about us, but we still have to learn to do something with it; though the elements of identity are 'given', we have to learn to use them. And some of the elements will be our personal achievement.

Thus, when we say that identity is constituted in core roles, this does not mean that is simple to discover what this identity is. For the simpler kinds of collective, this may be the case; but for individuals and for complex collective agents, identity has to be invented. The elements have to be combined melodically, given a style and an aesthetic whole, in an environment of others who are doing the same thing.

Something of the nature of this performance can be understood by reflecting on a passage from Henry James:

I remember an English novelist, a woman of genius, telling me that she was much commended for the impression she had managed to give in one of her tales of the nature and way of life of the French Protestant youth. She had been asked where she had learnt so much about this recondite being, she had been congratulated on her peculiar opportunities. These opportunities consisted in her having once, in Paris, as she ascended a staircase, passed an open door where, in the household of a *pasteur*, some of the young Protestants were seated at a table round a finished meal. The glimpse made a picture; it lasted only a moment; but that moment was experience...She knew what youth was, and what Protestantism; she also had the advantage of having seen what it was to be French, so that she converted these ideas into a concrete image and produced a reality...The power to guess the unseen from the seen, to trace the implication of things, to judge the whole piece by the pattern, the condition of feeling life in general so completely that you are well on your way to knowing any particular corner of it — this cluster of gifts may almost be said to constitute experience. (James, 1968: 86)

In the work of fiction, the implications of social setting and social facts have to be seen as character and incident. When the relations are correctly perceived, character is clarified and the hesitation of innumerable false starts vanishes. I shall quote James once more.

...there is an old-fashioned distinction between the novel of character and the novel of incident which must have cost many a smile to the intending fabulist who was at all keen about his work...What is character but the determination of incident? What is incident but the illustration of character? (p. 88)

One might add, what are character and incident but the drawing out of implications? In the course of this elaboration, the person behaves recursively, taking his construction of himself as a datum for elaboration. Kelly refers to this property of recursiveness when he writes:

> The self...can now be used as a thing, a datum, or an item in the context of a superordinate construct....When the person begins to use himself as a datum in forming constructs, exciting things begin to happen. He finds that the constructs he forms operate as rigorous controls upon his behaviour. (Kelly, 1955: 131)

Self constructs may start in ideological givens – and even these have to be worked through – but it is a restricted society in which large numbers of people end their search there, or fear those who attempt to go beyond the given. One of the forms that such fear takes is censorship of art and an encouragement of 'realism' – by which is meant stereotyped forms of work – since it is in art that men experiment with new forms of identity. It is in fiction, drama, sculpture, painting, architecture, that we see the implications of new conceptions of man. In fiction, particularly, identity is confirmed or questioned, by exhibiting the implications of identity experiments.

The false starts of the writer end in the waste paper basket. We are not shown the efforts by which he had to find the actions that are implied by his characters, or the characters that are implied by his actions. In our own lives, we are only too aware of the problem, of the false starts which we cannot throw into the waste paper basket. Often, we have to live with the consequences of a false action which we feel to be out of character, an action which has betrayed the identity we believe to be ours.

In its more static moments, life, like fiction, treads the same routine over and over again. This is what you want to be, one seems to be told repeatedly. This is what is meant by an ending. This is the inevitable consequence of what you are. In Kelly's terms the self taken as a datum now rigorously controls behaviour; and if the self is construed as an object, as a fixed thing, then life becomes mechanical and repetitive.

The implications of a mechanical self may be the death of spontaneity. Resistance to implications is often evident in the dialogue a person conducts with himself. 'I am not like that!' he protests. Or: 'I detest myself:' Or: 'What a splendid fellow you are!' Irony, reprimand, anger, shame, colour the relations which a person has with his identity.

Where self is categorically construed as a closed system, its implications may be impossible to avoid. The person finds his psychological processes channelled along predetermined paths.

Many men have sought to avoid the implications of the identities that are thrust upon them, as they see it, by a deliberate cultivation of disorder and the use of both non-rational and irrational modes. To the categorical self there is opposed a categorical anti-self, which caricatures it. In terms of Kelly's (1955) dichotomy corollary, we find the person choosing to elaborate the implicit poles of his core constructs, as an anti-self which may alternate with his self.

The cultivation may be 'deliberate', as Rimbaud's was when he cultivated *dérèglement de tous les sens* in his unsuccessful attempts to evade himself. The language of the anti-self is opposed to the language of the self. Where the language of the self is prose, that of the anti-self is poetry (or worse); where the self is excessively ordered and logical, the anti-self is disorderly and illogical; where the self is respectful and oppressed by duty, the anti-self is rebellious and neglectful of obligation.

Men systematically transform constructions of reality in wit and humour; they systematically transfer categorical or pre-emptive self constructs into the lived caricatures of personality disturbance and mental illness. Anti-selves caricature an oppressive society — in the sense that they turn the masks of the ideal inside out and upside down. Freud's hysterical patients caricatured, in their categorical anti-selves, the categorical selves they could not evade.

The anti-self of the chaotic and anxious person is an Absolute Other to whom he can offer himself, as believer, as penitent, as sinner, as impotent subject. Every system of 'true' identities (religious or political) contains models of selves through which security may be obtained.

The more the self is opened up to change, the more difficult it is to grasp who one is. That is the other side of the difficulty of the oppressively ordered self. What may result is simply confusion. Where we construe the self tightly, we are bound within narrow limits of action. Where we construe it too loosely, we have no direction.

There has to be enough structure for implications to be worked out.

The concept of working out the implications of identity relates to the concept of authenticity, which refers to acknowledging the implications of one's identity and acting on them.

Let us look firstly at authenticity as acknowledging the implications of one's identity.

Identity is always puzzling: the implications are half-grasped, seen dimly. To be authentic though, is to grasp those half-seen implications. There is no limit to the imaginativeness with which we may derive the implications of our identity, but these implications must be truly derived. That is, they must not be elaborations which conceal simple necessities.

Men who refuse the implications of their identity attempt to become *others*. Kelly defines the experience of guilt as the awareness of the dislodgement of the self from its core role structures (1955). Where this dislodgement cannot be reversed, the person is an *other* to himself. Marion Renard, in a review of Tristan's *Journal d'un Autre*, reminds us of some of the writers who have desired to be others. There is Nerval, Rimbaud and Tristan himself.

Here are only false trails, games of mirrors, false perspectives. No narrator to guide the lost reader in the labyrinth. And the personages which successively appear merely lead one to dead ends...'Who will prove that the "I" is my self and not a phantasm of my self?' one of the personages of *Birth of a Spectre* asks. (Renard, 1975).

Why should a person choose to become an other? To answer this we have to look at the implications of *otherness* as opposed to selfness in the constructs relating to identity. When some of the implications of an identity are too threatening, they may be averted by becoming an other. Nevertheless, the attempt does not usually succeed. One cannot become an other, except in madness. But if one cannot become an other, one might practise deception and behave and write as though one were. One drags one's identity about like a decaying corpse. If one gives up the attempt to be an other, one might try to change one's identity. This can only be done by acting truthfully on the implications of the self, by grasping it as a set of implications and being transformed by following those implications through. It is here that breakdown often occurs, that the implications cannot be followed through, and persons who cannot face these implications try to evade the consequences of being themselves by loosening their constructions of their selves. When these have been sufficiently loosened, there are no implications. There are various logics for loosening the self and evading implications: they are irony, mockery, symptom formation (being sick), condensation, displacement, distortion, confabulation, and the substitution of 'fantastic universals' for symbols of reality.

One remains one's self irrationally when one cannot remain one's self rationally.

Implications have to be grasped to be acted upon. Often, an implication *is* an action, as Luther pointed out in his ninety-five theses, nailed to the door of the Castle Church in

Wittenberg on 31 October 1571. The first thesis states:

1. Our Lord and Master Jesus Christ, in saying 'Repent ye, etc.,' meant the whole life of the faithful to be an act of repentance.

And the penultimate thesis reads:

94. Christians are to endeavour to follow Christ, their head, through pains, deaths, and hells.

When implications are truly derived the system of appearances becomes, like a well-spoken utterance, an indivisible composition.

The history of any complex system of life, such as Christianity, shows that the content of identity and even its categories (are priests necessary? a pope? are there Saints?) are continually revised in an attempt to cope with the problems of the time. This applies equally to political ideologies such as Marxism or nationalism. What I shall be showing, in a later section, is an example of an attempt to draw out the implications of an identity frame in the political programme of a party.

In considering how it is that men can sometimes negotiate new identities, we should bear in mind the following:

1   The elements of identity (like the vocabulary of a language) are not as determinate as we sometimes believe. Revision of dictionaries is interminable. Similarly, new identity markers are continually thrown up in the turmoil of social existence.
2   Rule systems can generate indefinitely large and sometimes infinite varieties of forms. Using rule systems as a model, and abandoning the notion that identity is simply a mask which is slipped on, we see how, given a finite set of elements and rules, an indefinitely large number of things can be done. This is not to say that such systems account for the way in which we produce 'identity-

sentences': they cannot. They describe structure, not production.
3 The fact that men take the actions of others into account means that they are 'open systems'.

As a consequence of these conditions and of the fact that identity is negotiated and monitored, it is both problematic and changing.

This is especially so if we bear in mind the factors of selection by competition and the resources of open and closed ideology.

This leads to the next implication.

DENSITY AND PRESSURE TO CHANGE

The greater the number of social agents competing for the same finite resources in the same way, the greater the pressure to change.

We could put this another way, and say that someone with a new way of doing things, a new 'act', stands a better chance of getting what he wants than a person who simply does what many others are doing, often superlatively well. Think of new art movements, new literary forms, new science, new fashions in clothes and cars. The market for the old art, the old literature, old science and old fashions is saturated. It is impossible for a young man to achieve pre-eminence simply by doing what his elders are already doing. The fiercely competitive will, therefore, attempt to get at scarce resources (wealth, admiration, power) by introducing new ways of doing things. In the course of this, new movements with an identity which is sharply differentiated from the old are created. It is not merely a matter of placing new goods on the market and seeing what will happen. That will not ensure the self-esteem of the new movement. The established order is mocked and attacked. The psychoanalysts attacked established psychiatrists (and were attacked by them); the analysts distinguish themselves sharply from the psychoanalysts; the dadaists mock academic art and middle-class values; Maoists mock the communist establishment; and so forth.

These processes are of the very greatest importance in politics. It is sometimes possible for an ambitious man to rise through existing parties, but often enough the really large changes are brought about by men who exploit needs which no established party can accommodate. Hitler is a remarkable example of this. The rise of disruptive ethnic movements where, superficially at least, there are adequate political means for the expression of views and the achievement of purpose is a common phenomenon. It is not so much that ethnic needs are not being satisfied as the fact that a niche exists in the power structure which is as yet unexploited that gives such movements their momentum. Entrepreneurs of political distinctions can work on substantial grievances to produce a movement which will carry them to power. The more this is an authentic vision, a 'disinterested' task, the more successful they are likely to be, finding exactly the right intonation, the right words, the right style.

REVOLUTION AND EVOLUTION

Tajfel (1978) points out that where existing groups with a preferred social identity can be joined by qualified members from less preferred groups, the existing system of social identities will be maintained and the existing ideology supported. Where joining is not possible, the challenge to the ruling groups is likely to be stronger once the legitimacy of the social order is questioned. Factors such as the collapse of an ideology in other countries, war, news, the failure of the ruling classes to perform their central functions, a relative rise in the self-esteem of the excluded class (due to better performance or comparison with like people in other countries and capacity to wring concessions out of those who rule), will contribute to questioning the legitimacy of a social order.

It follows from what I have said about negotiating and

monitoring identity (assumption 1) and competition (assumption 2) that persons will attempt to achieve a favoured social identity. Where this can be achieved by mobility, able members of the less favoured classes will tend to take this step. But this is no more than a tendency, and must be qualified by what I have said about competition. To what extent can the existing order provide for the most ambitious of the new talents? Would they not be better off exploiting some new opening in society — say, by rallying the class from which they came?

Equally interesting is the political and ideological entrepreneur who, because he is an outsider in his own, superior class, finds a way to power by recruiting agents from an inferior class. Many middle-class leaders who have espoused the cause of the working class have done precisely this. To say this is not to discredit their motives, but to attempt to account for a common phenomenon. The outsider in his own class places himself at the head of a class which is, as a whole, outside the privileged order. His behaviour is identical with that of any entrepreneur or innovator in commerce, art or science who creates a new form of life and finds a hitherto unexploited niche in society.

The rate of innovation is influenced by both competition and the degree of openness or closedness of ideology; it is also affected by what I have called 'richness' — the syntax and variety of elements in an ideology. What resources does the ideology make available to men who wish to change, nor merely from one pre-existing category to another, but the very categories of society? New forms of engineering, of healing, new professions, new forms of art are created. Of course, they have their place in a complex system by analogy and metaphor. They can be related to what has gone before. It is the richness of the enterprise that matters in modulating change.

Again, it is worth contrasting Sparta and Athens. In the former, the roles of the soldier, the helot and the soldier's farm-managing wife were rigidly prescribed. The society was designed against change. In the latter, many roles were open to men. The Spartan ideal was resurrected in a modified form in Plato's *Republic*.

By contrast, doctrines of 'incrementalism', 'pragmatism' and 'empiricism' in their various forms are against Utopia. They are tentative and unfinished. Fallibility is assumed; experiment is regarded as an essential path to improved knowledge. The state and other authorities can be challenged because their wisdom is not complete.

This means the protection of variety against uniformity, of inquiry against dogma, and of experiment against revelation.

Always, though, we seem to act within the limits of ideology, and this is the subject of the next chapter.

3
Ideology and Identity

In this chapter I shall do three things. The first is to examine the nature of ideology; the second is to see how ideological apparatus can be used to determine identity; and the third is to examine identity frames and traps.

What is ideology?

A lively way of taking up the subject is to look at the things Marx had to say about the engagement of men and groups in a struggle for ideas and principles, in *The Eighteenth Brumaire of Louis Bonaparte*. I shall quote a number of passages to show how Marx makes various points.

The first point is that men live metaphorically, borrowing identities to give significance and intelligibility to their actions, by fitting them into a framework of history. Here are Marx's words on this:

Hegel remarks somewhere that all the great events and characters of world history occur, so to speak, twice. He forgot to add: the first time as tragedy, the second as farce . . .The tradition of the dead generations weighs like a nightmare on the minds of the living. And, just when they appear to be engaged in the revolutionary transformation of themselves and their material surroundings, in the creation of something which does not yet exist, precisely in such epochs of revolutionary crisis they timidly conjure up the spirits of the past to help them; they borrow their names, slogans and costumes so as to stage the new world-historical scene in this venerable disguise and borrowed language. Luther put on the mask of the apostle Paul; the Revolution of 1789—1814 draped itself alternatively as the Roman Republic and the Roman Empire; and the revolution of 1848 knew no better than to parody at some points 1789 and at others the revolutionary traditions of 1793—5... If we reflect on this process of world-historical necromancy, we see at once a salient distinction. Camille Desmoulins, Danton, Robespierre, Saint-Just and Napoleon, the heroes of the old French Revolution, as well as its parties and masses, accomplished the task of their epoch, which was the emancipation and establishment of modern bourgeois society, in Roman costume and with Roman slogans... A century earlier, in the same way but at a different stage of development, Cromwell and the English people had borrowed for their bourgeois revolution the language, passions, and illusions of the Old Testament. When the actual goal had been reached, when the bourgeois transformation of English society had been accomplished, Locke drove out Habbakuk. (Marx, 1973: 146)

Then Marx asks the question:

Was it nothing but the fleur-de-lis and the tricolour, the House of Bourbon and the House of Orleans, the different shades of royalism, which held the fractions fast to their pretenders and apart from each other? Was it their royalist creed at all? (p. 173).

He replies that legitimate monarchy was the expression of *landed property*; the July monarchy was the expression of the rule of the 'bourgeois parvenus' of high finance, industry, capital.

It was therefore not so-called principles which kept these fractions divided, but rather their material conditions of existence, two distinct sorts of property... (p. 173).

Furthermore, feelings, convictions and 'modes of thought'

IDEOLOGY AND IDENTITY 45

arise on the basis of 'the different forms of property' (p. 173). What is the place of the individual in a class which has come to share these? He

may well imagine that they form the real determinants and the starting-point of his activity. (p. 174)

The individual is constituted, by tradition and upbringing, in a particular way. Later, I shall examine some of the processes at work in this structuration.

Marx poses a further question, of great significance for Mannheim's subsequent attempts to grant a privileged perspective to the 'free-floating intelligentsia'. What is the relation between a class and its apologists — those politicians, pamphleteers, teachers, philosophers or writers of fiction who speak for it? Do all those who advocate democratic reform in the France of 1848 (and in other revolutionary times) belong to the class of 'shopkeepers or their enthusiastic supporters' (p. 176)?

The answer Marx gives is that the intellectual representatives of a class are restricted in the same ways as those they represent

and they are therefore driven in theory to the same problems and solutions... (pp. 176–7).

There are several elements in these various passages that are important for our analysis of the nature of ideology.

The first is the assertion that material conditions of existence are the foundation of ideology. An ideology is cogent only to the extent that it gives an account of these real conditions, however transformed and disguised and dramatized the account may be. It seems that we like to have our explanations with a rich seasoning of drama. But even where the borrowings are strange — the Roman masks of Republican Europe and Imperial Britain — their cogency depends on inner content, on the way they capture the identities of the men whose credulity is engaged. There are exaggerations and failures, which are mere academic portraits in an old idiom, and which do not give the actors the metaphors they need for their present action. These fall away after a brief time, and the period in which they were exhibited seems to us to be a crabbed and lifeless one.

The second element is the way in which ideologies take mutually reinforcing forms. We find abstract theory, philosophy and history for the academics of the party as well as anecdote, slogan, legend and stories of heroes for ordinary men, newspapers and political practitioners of all sorts. The different forms which ideologies take are not simply the result of popularization, though. There are also forms which are appropriate to the various kinds of action in which men engage. The form which is appropriate for political action is not necessarily the form which is appropriate for friendship or family life. Relations between individuals may require anecdotes and myths which are different from those required by politics. An individual may have his difficulties explained to him in the story of the Oedipus complex or the conflict of Parent, Child and Adult (Berne, 1967); a class may have its problems explained in terms of the relations between capitalists and proletarians. In rich and coherent ideologies, such as Christianity in one of its several forms, there are versions for all levels of human interaction. There is Thomas Aquinas for the initiates and the Parables and *Pilgrim's Progress* for those in need of models. There is also the secular Christianity of Samuel Smiles for the young commercial. Ideology is closely associated with practices which are appropriate to various kinds of human relationship. In the present study, I am most concerned with political ideology, with the accounts men give of their political relations with each other. If the view put forward here is correct, there is usually some general agreement between different planes of ideology, though where there are contradictions, a considerable time may elapse before these are felt. Where there is fragmentation, it is not accidental. It is brought about by social conditions which contradict the dominant ideology, which then becomes a lifeless, a merely 'official' story, while men turn to all sorts of novel views in their attempts to achieve coherence.

The third important element in Marx's discussion above is that the individual then imagines that his *own* feelings and ideas are the cause of his actions. This is the point of view of psychological and psychiatric treatments as well, though it is admitted that the real problems often occur when people return to their own home and work environment. Of course the individual's feelings and ideas contribute to his action, but in what sense can we enlarge our understanding of society by starting with the individual? There is an interesting convergence here between Marxism and Skinnerian behaviourism, according to which we understand the individual by understanding the contingencies of reinforcement under which he has operated. Little is to be gained by looking into the individual and listening to his own account of himself, unless this account is understood in terms of the social contingencies under which it has formed. The individual person does not understand himself — not because of some intrinsic compartmentalization of mind, but because he does not understand the contingencies under which his thoughts, customs and impulses have been formed.

Marx discovers the essence of man in the structure of society, not in the individual. The key to this is the 6th thesis on Feuerbach.

Feuerbach resolves the religious question into the *human* essence. But the human essence is no abstraction inherent in each single individual. In its reality it is the ensemble of social relations. (Marx, 1975: 423)

The implications of this view will be discussed towards the end of this book when we ask whether psychology is a necessary science.

The fourth element is that people believe in the generality of their ideological solutions. People experience themselves — in their various transactions — and naturally take this experience to show what human beings are. From this experience — which is a blend of practice and ideology, of activity and explanation of that activity — they derive a general view of human identity and passionately defend this view because the questioning of it leads to anxiety. We should not take the vulgar view that ideology is defended only because it is in the material interests of individuals to do so. Ideology is based on the material conditions of society, but the relation is a complex one. When we see individuals defending an ideology it is often because they believe that the alternative is chaos, an undoing of themselves as persons, an annihilation of their identity. They preserve the practices of their society because these preserve their identity. The argument that they can remain whatever they are even if society changes is nonsense, because the participants see things in terms of their *attachments* to various institutions and practices. Of course, no group of people can hang onto their identity, but they may give themselves the impression that they are doing so by preserving certain core activities — such as consulting a sacred text, keeping a religion alive, speaking a given language, and regulating the introduction of changes through their own leaders.

Ideology is a 'way of life' and it is in this sense that I understand 'material conditions of existence'. The term 'material' is a mystification determined by an equally mystifying opposite — 'spiritual', where this is understood in the feeble sense of 'let them eat cake' if they can't have bread; or 'let them turn their minds to higher things' if their conditions of life are intolerable. A way of life is not possible without material means; it is conditioned by our natural history. We must earn our bread, but the desire to eat larks' tongues transforms the act of nourishing the body into a search for distinction. One cannot speak of such activities as determined by the material conditions of existence. They are human inventions which we can evaluate as we evaluate other human inventions, such as television, books, luxury cars, or castles.

The four elements described above are important in grasping the social role of ideology, in understanding how individual constructions of self and situation have a social provenance.

When we grasp these elements, we can understand why ideologies have the characteristics outlined by Alasdair MacIntyre. He writes:

I take any ideology to have three key features. The first is that it attempts to delineate certain general characteristics of nature or society or both, characteristics which do not belong only to the changing world which can be investigated only by empirical inquiry... The second central feature of any ideology is an account of the relationship between what is the case and how we ought to act, between the nature of the world and that of morals, politics, and other guides to conduct... The third defining property of an ideology is that it is not merely believed by the members of a given social group, but believed in such a way that it at least partially defines for them their social existence... a good deal of ideology not only overlaps with the proper concerns of sociology, but *is* sociology. (MacIntyre, 1971: 5–7)

We believe in the generality of our solutions because we experience ourselves as typically (or even ideally) human; and since each one of us is the case for himself, and since we are typical or even ideal, our beliefs are normative, and general, and appropriate as guides for others.

Marx indicated the mystifications that are to be found in ideologies. Liberalism exalts the individual and his property and proposes to protect him from any encroachments on either; yet the vast majority of mankind do not have property and are not able to live out the fine implications of the liberal state. People are urged to find the meaning of their lives in concepts which mystify their daily lives. The mystery may become a central feature of an ideology in which two planes of existence — a material and a spiritual — are opposed. What is mysterious at the material plane is explained on the spiritual plane. Secular ideologies must clear up their mystery on the material plane, and it is this that distinguishes them from religions. Men always live through this confusion, and it is in this confusion that they have to discover themselves. Though they may never achieve the whole thing, there are always discoveries to be made — or denied — and these discoveries are the steps in the achievement of authentic identity, by which we mean an identity that is not self-contradictory. Many ready-made masks are held out to us, there are many invitations to become the obvious, and there are many bewildering offers of salvation in this world or the next, but most of these masks are made by other men for other men. An ideology is a system of ideas adapted to the lives of some particular group of people, with some particular identity or set of identities. A general system, such as Christianity, or liberalism, or nationalism, comes to have a particular shape in a particular time and place, where it meets specific problems. It becomes the ruling ideology when the problems it meets are those of the most powerful class. The most subtle ideologies are not merely accommodations to greed, or to the simplest needs of people, though. They must solve the problems of existence, of the meaning of life, of the meaning of the social order, and in doing these things they may make demands on all members of society. The corruption or nobility of an age can be seen in the way men represent themselves and their relation to the world.

It seems obvious from such an analysis of ideology that it is no way to truth. It reflects material conditions; it is a superstition that our views on life are our 'own': 'the whole class creates and forms these out of its material foundation and the corresponding social relations' (Marx, 1973: 174). This leads to a difficulty.

It is no longer the exclusive privilege of socialist thinkers to trace bourgeois thought to ideological foundations and thereby to discredit it. Nowadays groups of every standpoint use this weapon against all the rest. As a result we are entering upon a new epoch in social and intellectual development... The truth of Max Weber's words becomes more clear as time goes on: 'The materialist conception of history is not to be compared to a cab that one can enter or alight from at will', for once they enter it, even the revolutionaries themselves are not free to leave it. (Mannheim, 1936: 66–7)

There are several difficulties with the 'reflection' theory that the whole of the superstructure, including philosophical ideas and political ideology, is a product of the economic base of society. How are we to distinguish between ideas? If all are simply products, then we have no way of choosing. There would be no way to distinguish between social theory — including Marxism — and ideology. The arguments about this are more confusing than enlightening. Althusser and Balibar (1975) argue that theory is not part of the superstructure, and that it may begin in ideology but that it develops beyond ideology. They are alarmed by Gramsci's failure to see a difference between religion and Marxism. Marxism is a science, they protest. But how does this protest rescue science from the position of being a 'product' or a 'reflection' of the economic base? The principal argument is that: 'Marx never, except in writings of his youth (and in particular in the manuscripts of '44), included scientific knowledge in the ideological superstructure' (Althusser and Balibar, 1975: 169). Of course, one can appreciate the dilemma even if one does not allow the reasoning. There *has* to be a way out for Marxism, if it is not to be like other theories (which are disguised ideologies). In most contemporary Marxist analyses, the view is taken that ideology and social theory necessarily reflect class position and are, therefore, necessarily partisan. Marxist theory has the advantage of being both partisan and right; and it achieves this interesting position by the following means. Each new class tries to give its ideas a broader base; hence there finally emerges a class which represents the interests of all. This leads to the abolition of contradictions and of classes (Jaworskyj, 1967).

But how is one to judge the broadening of the base and the elimination of contradictions? And will this be accomplished inevitably? *Must* each new class broaden the base of its ideas and what is the evidence that this is happening? In other words, this is an article of faith. 'Broadening of the base' seems to mean, quite often, liquidating the opposition.

Marx tried to distinguish between his views and speculative philosophy by introducing the notion of 'praxis' in his *Theses on Feuerbach*.

Thesis I:

The chief defect of all hitherto existing materialism (that of Feuerbach included) is that the thing, reality, sensuousness, is conceived only in the form of the *object or of contemplation*, but not as sensuous human activity, practice, not subjectively...

Thesis II:

The question whether objective truth can be attributed to human thinking is not a question of theory but is a *practical* question...

Theory XI:

The philosophers have only *interpreted* the world, in various ways; the point is to *change* it. (Marx, 1975: 421–3)

What he says here is true of political ideology. Political ideologies are normative — they lead to action, to change. It is also true of religion. There is no basis of distinction between ideology and evangelizing Christianity in these statements, nor in the concept of praxis — 'man's forming and grasping of himself and of nature by producing objects'. This was what the ascetics warned against, in turning men against the world. One can observe that Marx introduced into philosophy what was standard practice in politics and religion.

There is a conflict between the Marxist wish to explain everything in terms of the real relations of production and a wish to establish the privileged perspective of Marxist theory.

The problem which arises from this is: if our thought 'reflects' material conditions, is a social science possible?

We could take this question to mean several things, the first being that, since all thought can be traced to its ideological and hence material foundations, there is no reason to prefer one system of thought to the next. The answer to this is partly given in Russell's distinction between philosophies which are conceived as guides to action and the logic of these philosophies (1961: 752–3). We need guides to action and much of our thinking – whether we call it philosophy, social science or ideology – is of this kind. We may sometimes be able to show how these systems of thought are related to the material circumstances of the thinkers who produce them, since men always start from some position in society. But when we look at the details of their thought – its cohesion, clarity, logic, and the well-formedness of the arguments contained in it – then it is less clear how these are related to the 'material foundations' of their lives in any interesting way. All thinkers do, of course, exist as material beings. That said, we haven't achieved very much.

The methods of science are designed to correct individual prejudice, and for this reason we cannot distinguish capitalist science from socialist, Christian or atheist science. The methods are technical achievements. The application of science to human purposes is more clearly related to the economic and material foundations of society, by way of ideology, but the logic of scientific practice and thinking is not.

If these arguments are correct, there is no reason why a

social science should be limited by its ideological origins. Every social science will begin in ideology; that is to say, questions of 'programme' will be confused with questions of 'truth' and logic. When we discuss ideologies we are inclined to confuse what is desirable with what is true.

Nor are all ideologies equal. Some solve critical problems of the time — problems which are not imaginary, which are 'urgent' in the various meanings of the term. The survival of society may be threatened unless certain problems can be ideologically resolved. Ideologies must deal with plausible solutions to significant problems, and they must, in the process, engage the sensibilities of the time. They have an aesthetic as well as a rational dimension. People must see themselves as being able to take part in the kind of action required by the ideology. They must personally interpret the meaning of the resolution which the ideology promises and it must seem to them to be some kind of salvation.

Social science should be, not merely another ideology, but a science of ideology, able to comment on the relations between ideology and its social foundations. The development of such a science does not depend on the existence of some neutral or privileged class of observers. It depends, principally, on a change of focus, and the recognition of its concern as being not the development of a new ideology but a view of the relation between ideology and society.

It may be quite true that, starting from some social positions, men find it easier to develop good methods and good problems than they do starting from other positions; but the history of science shows that, once a science is beyond the folk wisdom stage, it must develop its own methods and its own problems. It then becomes the activity of a new class of men with an ideology appropriate to the practice of their scientific enterprise.

Yet we find ourselves in a new trap. We have appealed to the methods and practice of science, without being certain that the foundation of science is any firmer than that of ideology. Have we any reason to suppose that we will create a social science which will deliver more than relative knowledge?

Consider recent changes in the philosophy of science. On the one hand, there is the view, very much under attack, that can be described as positivism. It consists of the following broadly described beliefs and attitudes:
— the reality of the world is independent of the observer.
— perception is a direct link between the inquirer and the world.
— there are observation terms which are independent of theory.
— scientific practice is rational.
— knowledge is cumulative.
— logic is absolute and is discovered, not invented.
(See Phillips, 1977: 63).

A second view, which has considerable force today, regards science as depending on *paradigms* (Kuhn, 1962; 1970). Paradigms are related to language games and, quite obviously, to the sociological concept of ideology, since a paradigm could be described as a ruling language game, or as a dominant ideology in the domain of scientific practice. Paradigms are, as I have cited Kuhn to say on a previous page, model experiments, exemplary solutions, scientific practices, instruments, conceptions about what problems are significant and what kinds of solutions are acceptable. Language games are also practices, such as greeting, doing arithmetic, practising a religion. But there is an uncountable variety of them. These activities are not arbitrary, they depend on our 'natural history' — the fact that we think; use language; and agree in many judgements, such as judgements of emotions, colour, pain and number.

The difficulty is this: when I say, there are ten pebbles on the table, are there ten in some objective sense independent of our existence? Assume no one knows what 'ten' is? Isn't 'ten' (and all the other terms in the description) a human invention? Why, then, do we bother to say things like this?

Because it is useful *and* because, *in* a particular language game, it is true. It is not arbitrary. Many men learn the language game and use it coherently and apply it consistently to reach agreement that there are ten pebbles. But, if we learnt some other way of doing things, would it make sense to say there are *really* ten pebbles? Who would there be to say it? Propositions belong to the universe of human discourse, not to the natural world.

The rules of truth are extended in various games. Norms such as coherence, refutability, correspondence, usefulness and fertility are not 'there' to be discovered. They are inventions. 'The mathematician is an inventor, not a discoverer' (Wittgenstein, 1967: 167).

If mathematicians (and other makers of logic) are inventors and not discoverers, how can we be sure of the distinction between logic and programme?

When we contrast the consequences of positivist and frame theories of knowledge we arrive at the following:

Positivists believe that we can arrive at absolute truths; that scientific theories picture the world as it objectively is; whereas frame theorists believe that knowledge exists in paradigms, and that no absolute truth is possible.

It seems, then, that our escape from ideology has not succeeded. We have a choice between positivism – of which we are suspicious because it neglects the facts of power, of the structuring of perception, of the role of human interests in gaining knowledge – and some sort of ideological theory.

A quick summary of the problems of paradigm theory will be offered in the following paragraphs.

The first problem is that knowledge must be relative, given the assumption that it is determined by paradigms. If a paradigm is not merely the start of knowledge, but the element within which it has its existence, then we cannot know anything outside it, within the domain of knowledge that it structures. Yet, if the theory is reflexive in any way, it must apply to itself. It must be a theory within a paradigm, which presumably is simply one of a number of possible competing paradigms. Positivism is, then, an equally possible way of looking at things, unless we have criteria of judgement which are outside competing paradigms. But where do these criteria come from? What is their status in theory? The relativization of knowledge then calls into question its own foundations, or we are faced with the contradiction that some things are absolutely true and stand outside the realm of scientific knowledge determined by paradigms. But if not all knowledge is determined by paradigms, then we must have a way of getting at this knowledge, and of achieving truths which are not relative. We, therefore face the following possibilities. If the theory is true then it is only one possible theory among many and, therefore, it cannot be exclusively true; nor would we have any way of knowing that it is true. If the theory is false, there is no reason to attach any significance to it. If the theory is partially true, then what is the extent of its truth?

The next problem, even assuming that the theory could be true and yet not self-contradictory (in some way not understood), is how to compare and evaluate paradigms. If this is not possible, then moving from one paradigm to another is a purely arbitrary affair. Since knowledge is gained within a paradigm, to compare two paradigms means that we have to do so within a third paradigm. But the third paradigm can only be compared to either of the first two only by means of additional paradigms. And so we are faced with an infinite regress in which every comparison and evaluation requires yet another paradigm. This is, of course, the problem of pattern recognition in a theory of categories.

We have encountered this problem before, in evaluating ideologies. Ideologies cannot be supposed to be complete, determine knowledge, and also to be comparable. Such a conception of them leads of necessity to the view that change is revolutionary and that revolutions are arbitrary.

The elimination of contradictions by the creation of a broader and broader ideology (or paradigm) which includes all others is, within this view, no more desirable than growing a larger and yet larger cabbage which finally fills the world. The cabbage is simply one plant among many possible plants; the ideology (or paradigm) is simply one among many. The broadening of the ideology is merely a matter of faith — one prefers cabbages to all other things. And, once the super-paradigm had been achieved, one would not be able to carry out the necessary tests to know whether one had achieved the best of all possible worlds or simply one of many possible worlds.

What would such a paradigm be like? Having achieved the ultimate, no deviation could be allowed since all deviations would, by definition, be regressions. Whereas the doctrine of positivism subordinates knowledge to the infinite variety of the world, the doctrine of the ultimate paradigm or ideology subordinates knowledge to particular human practices.

Even considered as a limiting case, it is a self-contradictory notion. A paradigm which fills the space of all available knowledge is no longer a paradigm but a universe. Among other universes? How would we know?

A consequence of this theory that knowledge is possible only within paradigms is a 'collective solipsism' (Phillips, 1977: 85) which maintains that worlds are accessible in quantum jumps only, as we change paradigms. Realities are separate.

The concept of paradigm takes Wittgenstein's *language games* to an unprofitable extreme, selecting a particular one as dominant and complete.

We can try putting it another way. Assume that the realm of meaning is created by human activity. When we talk of 'meaning' or 'logic' we are talking about human facts which cannot be given back to the natural world. On the other hand, the relation between the world of meaning and the natural world is not arbitrary: we have evolved in the natural world. In the course of this evolution, we have developed certain ways of engaging each other and the world. Each cognitive, sensory, or motor tool creates a new engagement. These *engagements* are to be thought of as 'sparking' particular realities, in the way that atomic particles reveal themselves in collision with each other. For us, reality exists as a set of possible engagements, some of which do not achieve what we expect or wish them to achieve, and some of which do. Some are incomprehensible, some are both predictable and intelligible. There are infinite though not arbitrary possibilities of engagement with the world and each other. The passive universe has disappeared. We have no way of looking at it through a transparent window. We create possible modes of existence by our engagements, our activities.

This removes attempts to picture the universe as the passive object of our inquiry. We attempt to anticipate what we do to it and what it does to us. Coherence often breaks down when we cross from one mode of activity to another. There are many engagements which cannot be reduced to a common denominator: natural science, art, religion, play. We must imagine a responsive universe of infinitely variable possibilities.

And so, paradigms begin to look like the special case. They refer to systems which are closed off and already too coherently structured. They are like the academic art and the complete physics that must be destroyed by impressionism and relativity theory.

The point is that paradigms, where they are active, are imperfect systems. Men who belong to a certain school are not identical, they have some features in common and differ in many others. This is the important fact that Wittgenstein drew attention to as 'family resemblances'. Practitioners of physics at a certain time are not more alike than chairs, tables or vehicles. They might, if arranged in a line, present (metaphorically) a continuum of viewpoints; but the extremes would be very different indeed. The fact that a paradigm (or an ideology) cannot by any stretch of the imagination be more than an idealized representation of a large number of very dissimilar events shows us why paradigms fail to hold together. It also shows us how men can compare them. They don't belong to the paradigm; they don't swallow it whole, they don't even care about it in many instances.

Some of these problems arise in theories of pattern recognition. How do we recognize that an 'a' is an a, a 'chair' is a chair? One possibility is to compare each particular 'a' to the ideal a (each 'dog' to Plato's dog as Russell, 1940, says). According to this theory, our recognition of 'a' is determined by the complete a, stored in Plato's heaven, just as our understanding of an event is determined within a complete paradigm. If, on the other hand, we argue that people use a large number of features to recognize 'a' and 'dog' and other objects, we quickly see how recognition becomes possible without an ideal. This has the advantages of dissolving the problem of categories referred to above.

Similarly, we can say that scientists who are working in a particular paradigm should be recognized as doing so (by the labouring scholar), not by reference to a perfect model of that paradigm (in which case we will be hard pressed to find any member of the category), but by virtue of their possessing *some* of the features which we use to describe the paradigm. In addition, each person will possess many features neglected by our description.

Our desperate attempts to get men to resemble each other succeed only to the extent required to keep things decent. In dress, in thought, in art, in science, the rule is difference as often as it is similarity: things are held together only long enough for the conscientious scholar to get his group portrait and for the even more conscientious scholar to point out that the picture is not quite true!

What is 'ideological apparatus'?

Though we have seen that it is wise to abate our claims concerning the extent to which consciousness, thought and content are constituted entirely within a particular ideology, it remains an interesting problem to examine the 'family resemblances' of those who have similar positions in society. They do not belong to a category, but they show many of the features and limitations of their position. How does this happen and how do they learn their lessons?

After the rather general remarks about structures which help to determine individual and collective agents in the preceding pages, it is well worth looking at a particular case: how does a part of the 'ideological apparatus' function to maintain an ideology? Is it simply a question of ideas which are so pervasive that no one is disposed to question them?

There certainly are 'ideas' of a sort attached to every social practice. 'A woman's place is in the home' is an excuse, a justification, a command and a prohibition, depending on its use. It explains, though to a smaller and smaller extent, why women are not to be found competing in occupations which require a considerable amount of training. 'It would be a waste.' Not only that, but women ought then to take up those occupations which are entailed by their identity as home-makers — teaching infants, nursing, social work, occupations in which warmth and sympathy and other feminine gifts are required. In addition, women as a group are prevented from undertaking jobs which require physical strength, though a particular woman may be strong enough. All this is commonplace. But is it the ideas that maintain the practice? The answer is that the ideas are part of the practice. They are a system of platitudes (which prevent further inquiry) and theories (which present the question in a mystifying way). The platitudes function in the manner of restricted codes (Bernstein, 1961) and appear to present facts of nature. The theories refer to the physiology of women and the psychology of children, who cannot do without their attention. 'There is no substitute for a mother's love.' Perhaps there isn't. That isn't the question. More to the point is whether mother can best give her love by remaining in the home.

Ideas about race have functioned in the same way. There are the platitudes ('they're like children') and the theories ('smaller cranial capacity') which justify discriminatory practices. (P. V. Tobias, 1972, surveys some of these.)

These ideas are, as I have said, part of the practice. We need to look at the total arrangement in which these ideas are actions — prohibitions, commands, explanations, excuses and justifications. We can gain a particularly clear impression of the way the ideological apparatus functions by examining institutions specifically designed to pass on knowledge — such as schools. There are several very important points, which can be generalized to other instruments of ideology.

The first important point is that we should not think of the school as simply passing on 'ideas', by indoctrination in explicit lessons. This kind of ideological socialization is probably the least effective way. The schools 'maintain order' — and conserve the structure of class relations (Bourdieu and Passeron, 1970). They do this in several ways. The first is internal: there is a strong separation of the pupils (who have to learn) and the instructors (who know). They exercise power through knowledge; knowledge becomes power. The relation between them is embodied in the separation of the teacher from his class and in the separation of the kinds of things they do: the one talks and tells the other, who listens and takes notes. The power of position and role has been experimentally investigated by Ross, Amabile and Steinmetz (1977), who have found that even incompetent persons who ask the questions are rated as more knowledgeable than competent persons who have to answer them. The very structure of communicating knowledge, therefore, legitimates authority. Another way in which schools — and universities — establish an attitude to authority is by means of a syllabus which defines valuable knowledge. What children know or are able to do outside the syllabus — even within the subject they are studying — is irrelevant to their evaluation, to their passing or failing.

The creation of a response to authority and the scale of values imposed on knowledge commences early and persists into university. There are, as a consequence, many who can learn very effectively what is required of them, but who cannot create knowledge. To create knowledge is to leave the order that has been created. This may explain why women, who have been most heavily leant on by authority, have been excellent learners and relatively poor innovators in many branches of knowledge.

One can summarize the effect of schooling as follows:

> The school does not inculcate opinions but dispositions to act and react, unconscious schemes on the basis of which thought and action is organized in various situations. By analogy with linguistic theory, Bourdieu and Passeron write that it is not a language which is learnt, but a generative grammar of attitudes. (Cot and Mounière, 1974, vol. 2: 85)

This was very well understood by Thomas Arnold, who became headmaster of Rugby in 1828 and greatly influenced the public schools of England and grammar schools which strove to imitate them. The purpose of education was to make a boy into a 'Christian, a gentleman and a scholar' in that order. These three purposes were happily combined in a system devoted to the study of dead languages and the Bible, a system which depended not merely on content but on form.

> He would treat the boys at Rugby as Jehovah had treated the Chosen People: he would found a theocracy; and there should be Judges in Israel. (Strachey, 1948: 197)

The school was governed by a hierarchy in which every

sixth-form boy was a 'praepostor', responsible to the Headmaster, who remained remote, 'involved in awful grandeur', and the impression he made upon younger children 'was of extreme fear' (p. 198).

What is interesting once more is the power of appropriate metaphor in the ordering of conduct and sentiment. The Testaments supplied examples of righteous conduct while the school embodied, with Arnold in the seat of judgement, the moral order of the world. The recondite and useless subjects which were taught were like the revelations of a mysterious deity. Daily life, no matter how intelligently lived, could not supply the boys with knowledge which would be of any value in that remote world. Its ways were as inscrutable as the ways of revelation.

The Romans and the Greeks supplied the metaphors of civic government. The power of these metaphors derived from their incorporation into the government of the school (praepostors blended into a theocracy!). In a modern school they might be studied as interesting stories; but in Arnold's school the study of the ancient texts was in itself a source of virtue. He made the fortunate discovery, at an early stage of his career, that the only subjects he was equipped to teach were the best means for forming both character and intellect. And so, for well over a century, Latin and Greek were thought to mould, shape and convey the life of reason in its most perfect form. The discipline of mastery, the long hours of postponed enjoyment, the final pleasure as meaning and perhaps even beauty trickled through the stone wall of the text, undoubtedly did have its effect on character. Within austere form there is the rich life of emotion.

One of the main functions of schools is that they convince the excluded classes that they have been legitimately excluded. This is one of Illich's complaints about 'schooling' and the use of irrelevant certificates and diplomas in excluding people from jobs. Those who have 'failed' at school often feel that it is quite reasonable that they should fail in life and not be considered for better salaries and better posts though they may be doing very well in the job. Nor can they be considered for further education, even if their failure is quite irrelevant.

Since many of those who fail are from the lower classes, the system legitimates their exclusion from posts for which they might otherwise qualify. Their failure also entitles them to receive less for whatever work they do, since they do not qualify for any diplomas or other signs of learning. In terms of the principles of distributive justice:

$$\frac{P\text{'s returns}}{P\text{'s investments}} \quad \text{should equal} \quad \frac{O\text{'s returns}}{O\text{'s investments}}$$

Where P's investments are smaller than those of O (he has less education) he is entitled to less, though the entitlement is arbitrary in terms of relevant accomplishment (Brown and Herrnstein, 1975).

Exclusion is effective while the school and the educated are the normative reference group. Propagandists such as Illich and Freire are among those who are attempting to change this, but they have to struggle against the conservatism of schools, universities and professions (often filled with people educated to a high level of incompetence). Much learning is conspicuous consumption disguised as relevant investment.

One of the effects of preventing people from getting credit for what they have learnt outside educational establishments is that they may not realize that they have learnt anything on their own. Absolute dispossession prevents awareness of dispossession, to paraphrase Cot and Mounière (1974).

The control of instruments which socialize individuals to accept the legitimacy of the prevailing order is called *symbolic force*. By symbolic force, meanings are imposed which conceal the very power relations on which they depend. There can be little doubt that the educational system is one of the most effective instruments of symbolic force, since it is the system in which children are prepared for the life they have to lead. In a factory society the schools are factories in which children are expected to perform meaningless and uninteresting tasks to a strict time schedule. Schools for the children of 'creative' parents are expected to let children discover and dabble. In 'closed' societies, children may spend most of their time reciting (not discussing) a sacred text.

There is nothing strange in all this. In most instances the structure of the school can be easily understood as a preparation for 'life'. What is interesting is that the 'theory of education' which surrounds the practice of the school generally takes the form of a universal theory – and is understood as fundamental and appropriate to all. It is a 'theory of education', not a 'theory of education for a factory society' or 'how to educate people not to question the sacred texts'. Individuals, as I have said before, experience themselves as prototypes of the human race. This universality and the mystification of it is the foundation of symbolic force.

Socialization effectively replaces force in the governing of society.

Persons acquire a social identity which is appropriate to the power structures of their society. They are responsive to its demands in a supple and adaptive way, because they have acquired 'a generative grammar of attitudes', a system of 'dispositions'.

Though I have concentrated on the educational system and the school in particular in these remarks about 'ideological apparatus', what I have said can be extended to almost every social organization, almost all of which 'socialize' those who enter them. Sometimes we have little choice in the matter. The patriarchal family structure (or, for that matter, the matriarchal family) embodied a relationship between men and women, adults and children. The effects of this on such events as 'oedipal conflict' and the formation of the superego are not yet clear. There are, naturally, ideas attached to such a structure. Even better, there is a discourse, a system of prohibitions and commands, gems of wisdom, apophthegms and moral summaries. Where does father sit at the table? Who carves the meat? Father pays for it all. Father knows best. Keep quiet when adults are talking. All that has gone by the board and new family structures, with their own ideas, are now in existence. Usually, they are coy about the matter of power, and mystification is as prevalent as ever.

The democratic family is extended to the human relations model of industry. The firm is a family, a happy one if possible, to which employees belong and in which they find their security and emotional satisfactions.

It is not necessary to multiply examples. The fundamental lesson is that societies aspire to moral government, in which consent replaces force. This is excellent. Consent is given by informed persons — carefully formed.

And that is the achievement of the 'ideological apparatus'.

Identity frames

Each ideology incorporates an identity frame, which is a paradigmatic set of identities used in accounting for events in a particular sphere of activity, such as politics, education, or religion. The identity frame is used by all those who share a given ideology, bearing in mind our previous remarks about 'family resemblance'. What is abstracted in constructing an identity frame is a composite portrait, a common pattern. We should avoid freezing the group and wondering how change could ever happen.

There are identity frames because we all have to make working assumptions, supported by convenient practices, about proper appearance and its entailments. A proper appearance must be supported by various material objects — an establishment of sorts: the coach and four, perhaps a harp and a sketch book, a carefully chosen volume of Horace, a parliamentary mace, the ark in the temple, seating arrangements in a lecture theatre, a Rolls Royce, a safety pin through the wing of a nostril, a distinctive scent, an explosive racket from the souped-up job, the studded belt and boots of a biker...

Experience has to be organized, accounts have to be intelligible, assumptions have to be made. Goffman develops Williams James' question 'under what circumstances do we think things are real?' as follows:

> I assume that definitions of a situation are built up in accordance with principles of organization which govern events — at least social ones — and our subjective involvement in them; frame is the word I use to refer to such of these basic elements as I am able to identify. This is my definition of frame. My phrase 'frame-analysis' is a slogan to refer to the examination in these terms of the organization of experience. (Goffman, 1975: 11)

The binding nature of even temporary frames is well known from the work of Zimbardo (1975) on simulated prisons, Milgram (1974) on obedience, and Asch (1956) on conformity.

In even the most conclusive ideologies there are different spheres of activity — sport and politics, art and religion — which means that there are, to say the least, different accounts. Sometimes these conflict with each other. One may note the annoyance of sportsmen who protest against 'introducing politics into sport'. Those to whom the religious life is dominant may attempt to impose its categories on politics and education. Nowadays, political life is more likely to be dominant, with the result that religion is absorbed by political problems in political terms. What is religion doing about poverty? about freedom fighters? about the advancement of democracy or some other political goal? A separation of virtue and politics is no longer possible, according to many. Religion must be 'socially and politically relevant', it must speak to the present needs of people before it can — if ever —

address them on their relation to the next world. Indeed, is there a next world? If there is, its outline is very faint — almost invisible — in the sketch of reality presented to the modern Church.

Attempts to cross and to defend the various domains of reality have always occurred. The political or religious relevance of art and education have been perennial subjects of dispute. Dominant world views require compatibility, if not complete congruence. One consequence of absorption is that we prepare the way for confrontations in which many of our identity frames are at stake at the same time, adding to a struggle in which logic and liquidation play an equal part.

The interpreters of ideology — usually themselves in the grip of the assumptions which they enact — offer a simple set of identities in a family of mutually reinforcing myths. The cigarette advertisement, the cowboy, the history of pioneers; the philosophy of racism and the myth of the civilized and the savage agree with a religion which interprets the world in terms of the elect and the damned. A flood of love stories, adventures, news items, political speeches, histories and philosophies drive home the same message.

The seductiveness of these offers lies in their existential as well as their material advantages. We are offered salvation, security, solidarity, superiority and a good bargain. We are offered a better understanding of our place in the world. We are offered meaning and a bond with others like ourselves. We are offered status and wealth and a justification for our conduct. And justifications are the backbone of strong identity. We half believe all of this; but there are times when, swept up in definite actions, we believe all of it. In any case, we are not offered opinions, we are offered scheme after scheme, richly enfolding us in fact and theory, in fiction and hard news. We lose the capacity to see what is not in the ideological family.

The power of this family of stories is that its promises are sometimes met. If they were never reinforced in practice, they would remain folk stories. Rather quaint. But they 'work' in complex ways, to explain and to secure our interests. They seem to deal with realities, as we understand them. They are the 'serious' equivalent of fotofiction.

As an example of ideological invitation, consider a speech by the South African prime minister, Dr H. Verwoerd, in the House of Assembly on 9 March 1960 during the budget vote. There is nothing extraordinary about the manner of this speech. One could find its equivalent in the speeches made every day by men who have to speak on the issues of the day to audiences who take their way of interpreting events for granted. What is offered is not so much an interpretation as a confirmation. A vast number of persons – even those who oppose what Dr Verwoerd says – take his identities for granted.

I feel that the role of the White man in the world is not receiving sufficient attention. It appears that a world psychosis has arisen of thinking only of the rights and privileges and freedoms of the non-whites, whilst in fact the White man is responsible for everything the Black man has in the way of ideals, ambitions and opportunities. I therefore consider it essential to emphasize that when one talks about merits one is not concerned only with the merits of persons, of individuals, but sometimes also with the merits of nations, communities and national groups. I shall have more to say in that regard.

Let us first look at the position of the White man in the world today. Forget the role he played in past centuries. In the world of today, in this atomic age, who is responsible for the developments and inventions, the discoveries and their application in various spheres?

The opposition of white and black identities as construed by Dr Verwoerd is not an illusion. It is a good example of a frame – of political and ideological realism. 'Realism' is one of the marks of ideology, and that is why there is not a mindless dictatorship in the world which does not plead for realism and reject deviations from it on grounds of 'lack of realism' or the 'undermining of tradition'.

Identity frames are indispensable. They are a fact of social coherence, elements of an ideological discourse which places subjects and their actions in relation to each other.

I wish to discuss three distinct identity traps which can occur as a consequence. I shall call them the squeeze, the con and the cuckoo. First, though: what is an identity trap?

An identity trap is an identity frame which cannot be negotiated in a social transaction. It allows too little room for manoeuvre, it pre-empts reality, denies other possibilities, and allows too little freedom. It fills the whole of social reality in a dogmatic and final way. It is black-and-white construing. Dr Verwoerd's speech is a good example of an identity trap. Since we are all black or white or non-white (which he goes on to mention), we are all drawn into his categories; we are all dragged into the picture he paints. It is difficult to refuse it altogether, to insist on an entirely different picture in which white and black are not the categories of social reality.

This concept of an identity trap leads straight to the first form of it: the squeeze.

THE SQUEEZE

One might call this the Procrustean bed.

Though we all require identity frames to think about social relations, some identity frames are picked up off the street, as it were, without reflection.

Sometimes there are very sound reasons for feeling trapped in an identity frame. A person may take full responsibility for the implications of a relationship in which she finds herself. She may be a mother, or a judge who has to act against the wishes of the government. She does not flinch from the obligations she imposes on herself as a mother or a judge in a particular situation.

On the other hand, she might be trapped because she has not inquired deeply enough, because she is ignorant of what she is doing, or because she is not sufficiently clever or courageous.

Persons whose view of reality is squeezed into a ready-made ideology often use a limited vocabulary in a mechanical way to describe their relations to events. 'Bourgeois revisionism', 'Trotskyite', 'dialectical materialism' and various citations from 'The Works' become the instruments of such comprehension as they manage. Nationalists describe all their problems in terms of ethnicity, communists see classes everywhere, and socialists rely on committees. What is noticeable is that for some the system becomes a caricature, a possible identity becomes the inevitable identity, and others are drawn into their systems. A racist converts others into racists, a dogmatic communist converts all others into either comrades or lackeys of the imperialists, the bourgeoisie and the capitalists.

Nothing is left of the subject except a category.

The individual subject has been placed at the disposal of God, of social structures, of ideology ('interpellated') and of the unconscious.

During the brief flowering of humanism, man was placed at the centre of his existence. The social yoke was lightly felt, the weight of an institutionalized God had been displaced for a brief moment. It was probably a mistake to claim too much for a realm of meaning which placed the individual at its centre. Yet though it may not be objectively true that man is the captain of his soul, the fact that he believes it makes a difference to the forms of government he is prepared to tolerate. The imagery of personal responsibility and personal freedom makes tyranny more difficult to maintain than the imagery of fatalism and despair does.

The excentration of the subject and the growth of the Other (with a capital) signifies the growth of an order of significance in which we are prepared for subordination to others.

Subordination may be more or less pernicious, depending on the nature of the other. Where it is mechanical (perhaps no more mysterious than a capital letter), we are subordinated to the tyranny of the commonplace — commonplace ideas, commonplace rulers. We may have our romance with a tractor.

How can we avoid being squeezed?

One way is to rely on parables which capture the essential dilemmas of mankind without attempting the detailed prescriptions which must be devised afresh in every new situation. Texts, histories and sacred writings have to be understood, interpreted and applied, not merely repeated and imitated. Enigmatic and profound figures provide the tools for a personal exploration of our relations to other human beings. The study of great figures provided these opportunities for reflection in the past: whom do we study now?

If we trivialize our conception of greatness we shall pay the price.

I shall now discuss the con.

THE CON

A con succeeds when we manoeuvre others into accepting an identity frame in which they are inferior to us. An identity con is one of the attempts rulers make to substitute symbolic for physical force.

Cons are best attempted from positions of power; they survive an equalization of power between the parties concerned for a very brief period, if at all. The identity con is similar to the task of selling the Empire State Building. It requires the same selection of information, the same management of impressions, but it has to be done on a massive scale to succeed politically. Missionaries, magistrates and ceremonial parades are not enough. The manners of invincible superiority must be backed by regiments and battleships. The generous raising of one's inferior to a position just a shade below one's self will be gratefully accepted only while he can be struck down for presuming too much.

The con of 'false consciousness' is well known to Marxists:

the working-class men who did not believe that members of the working class could govern; the colonized peoples who were only too happy to acquire the accent, the dress and the manners of the colonizers, hoping to pass themselves off as one of them or simply to manage some of the tokens of superiority (Fanon, 1970; Mannoni, 1956).

The incomplete con can leave the victim aware that he has been conned; the complete con can deprive him of even that awareness. Earlier, in discussing the ideological apparatus, I observed that symbolic force is an effective substitute for physical force. The colonized who are allowed to use some of the symbols of the colonizers may come to think of themselves as privileged (though they remain the butt of their superiors). They become almost Roman; or almost European.

The incomplete con does not require an external observer to interpret the 'real interests' of those who have been conned. Expressions of doubt and dismay are voiced by the victims themselves. The complete con, on the other hand, requires such interpretation. Activists have to point out to the conned that they could do better, that the position they have accepted is not the best bargain they could make, if only they would rely on their leaders and their native courage. The activist is helped by a theoretical stance, such as an appeal to 'the people', 'the nation', or 'the working class'.

From a nationalist position, an activist might show those who have bought the con that they have unique ethnic qualities — a language, a physique, a history that no one else has the privilege of sharing. He might also point out that there are certain definite political and material advantages to breaking frame. A Marxist might point out to a group of people that their position in the capitalist system is not a fact of nature, that it is not inevitable, and that there is another social order in which they might have both political and economic power, of a sort.

Where ethnic and class divisions coincide, nationalist and Marxist theorists will clash on whether they are confronted with a 'racial', an 'ethnic', or a 'class' conflict. Much thought may be expended on this question, raising the spectre of Kuhn's incommensurable paradigms.

I became personally aware of the effectiveness of the British con when, in 1968, a Chinese from Hong Kong spoke admiringly of British exploits in Zululand. It was winter, American accents were all about us in Boston, and we had both been educated by Scottish schoolmasters, and comics like *Champion* and *Wizard*. The Americans knew nothing of these things. Several of them placed Zululand on the borders of Nigeria. Others had no reverence for the British Empire. Of course, the mere shell of Empire was all that was left. It had degenerated into a Commonwealth, but with my companion from Hong Kong we did a tour of the ruins. The symbols were still powerful; the red coats evocative; Biggles on the wing; all's right with the world.

The English had been a *nomic* majority whose confident superiority (surviving in comic strips and boys' weeklies) had left elbow-room for others. Like the Bostonians of Henry James's America, we had lived in the greater world of Europe while we went to school in Hong Kong and Potchefstroom. We had both come across relics of the British Empire who spoke of England as 'home' after an absence of forty years; those for whom Kipling had written:

> ...they shall return as strangers
> They shall remain as sons.

In South Africa, there were many who resisted the con, who were aware of the danger of accepting a place in a world in which they would be not quite equal. They knew, without resort to Marx (Calvin was enough), the extent of their economic, social and political inferiority under British rule. A separate language, a distinct religion, a pioneering life with its peculiar adaptations, were blended to the unique style of their struggle for power. Uniqueness and difference became the tools of their identity. The more they defined themselves by opposition, the more cohesive and exclusive their group identity became.

The history of the Afrikaners is the history of their refusal. The history of the blacks will, similarly, be a history of refusal. Every conquering power attempts to create a world within which others have their place; it requires overwhelming force to keep them there.

In contemporary South Africa we see the familiar picture of attempts to squeeze events into a frame, to con others into accepting this frame, and the renewed struggle of the politics of identity.

THE CUCKOO

This is an identity trap of considerable significance: it occurs when one identity begins to displace other identities from a person's repertoire. It is the squeeze carried to an extreme.

The person becomes a persona. She begins to behave as though life had only one significant part for her to play. Jung has some interesting things to say about this:

The person...is the individual's system of adaptation to, or the manner he assumes in dealing with the world. Every calling or profession, for example, has its characteristic persona...Only, the danger is that [people] become identical with their personae – the professor with his textbook, the tenor with his voice...One could say, with a little exaggeration, that the persona is that which in reality one is not, but which oneself as well as others think one is. (*Collected Works*, vol. 9: 122)

Erikson speaks of a weak ego which

seems to sell out to a compelling social prototype. A fake ego is established which suppresses rather than synthesizes those experiences and functions which endanger the 'front'. (Erikson, 1968: 59)

The woman who sells out to her persona is frightened. She

has an impoverished style in her relations with others because she cannot risk any other performance. She has succeeded as a professor — especially a professor who cannot be questioned and is an 'authority' inside the classroom and out — and she won't try anything else; perhaps because she doesn't know how, perhaps because the implications of being anything else are too frightening. If she is just a woman, like so many others, why isn't she a mother, a charming wife, a seductive mistress, an ornament in a sports car, or so many of the things she has come to believe a woman should be? The consequence is that she sticks to being a professor and becomes more and more lonely, unless she is lucky enough to be rescued by someone who refuses to believe that she is as limited or as dedicated as she imagines.

The cuckoo is politically important when it is consolidated in a political movement. Persons who find that they can play out their major identity on a large scale can become fanatical participants in extremist movements. They become the terrorist, the assassin, the patriot, the jingo, or the party member, with a devotion which is impossible for most ordinary people to understand. The process of consolidation supports an identity that has already begun to throw the others out of the nest.

Political movements do not depend exclusively on cuckoos. Politics has fallen into low repute — image has replaced character, charisma has thrown brilliance overboard — but there are political activities which depend on charm, persuasion, reasoning, integrity and even honesty. In such movements, men may attempt to expand the frames of human identity, to recognize the value of difference, and to provide means for the cultivation of new ways of life.

Such movements are, unfortunately, rare.

4
Identity Traps: A Frame and a Con

An identity frame, as I have already remarked, is a paradigmatic identity set which enables us to make sense of events by reference to the nature of the agents involved. A con is a more or less successful attempt to manoeuvre others into accepting our frame, even though it gives them a position which is inferior to ours.

The identities in the frame are known by categorizing and characterizing statements (Strawson, 1959). If we look back at Dr Verwoerd's speech, in the previous chapter, we see the categories easily enough: white, black, non-white. We see, also, that each of these categories has certain characteristics relating it to others: the whites are more innovative and creative than blacks are, to take one.

In referring to identity, we should realize that we are making both categorizing and characterizing statements. An identity frame consists of a set of categories and also a set of characteristics attached to these categories. A con gets others to support both.

Identities come in solar systems, with a reference identity in the position of the sun and the complements of the reference identity in the positions of the planets. To understand any identity frame (and, therefore, any identification), it is necessary to grasp both the reference identity and its complements. Identifying with Daddy, to take an example, means seeing complementary identities (Mummy, Jack, Jane, Uncle Henry and the servants) from his perspective. The characterization of *his* identity implies categorizing and characterizing them.

In public life, important reference identities consolidate the identities of collective agents. The enigmatic identities of Christ, Buddha, Marx and Gandhi are the foci of myths — powerful narratives in which significant relations between source types are portrayed. National heroes such as Lincoln, Joan of Arc, Bismarck, Garibaldi, and mythical figures such as the cowboy and the Voortrekker help us to define the core of our collective identity. As Bill Bloggs I may not be much, but as a member of the nation that bred one of these heroes I am a force to be reckoned with.

World views, such as Christianity, have well developed categories (saint, sinner, the Trinity, angel, devil, heathen, priest) which are related in complex ways (sinning, repenting, forgiving, punishing, judging, submission) with various results (salvation, damnation). These categories and the relations which characterize them are not merely stated; they are, like all things which grip us, rendered in narrative and visual art, in music and in poetry.

This is true, to a greater or lesser extent, of all systems of collective identity. Naturally, some are more inclusive than others; some embrace both this and other worlds.

The quality of our vision of man, society and the world is directly reflected in these images, which equip us against immediate self-interest and too narrow a vision. Philip Sidney contrasts visions of the ideal with subservience to 'fact':

For indeed Poetry ever setteth virtue so out in her best colours, making Fortune her well-waiting handmaid, that one must needs be enamoured of her...But the historian, being captivated to the truth of a foolish world, is many times a terror from well doing, and an encouragement to unbridled wickedness. (1922: 19–20)

Universal views take on peculiar local forms. The categories of Christianity — heathen and believer — were superimposed on a political and economic system of categories — native and colonizer — to yield the local categories and local characteristics of European expansion and slavery from the sixteenth to the nineteenth centuries.

The 'interests' which keep these identities in their 'proper places' are complex: they range from fear of destruction and loss of identity (not simply categorical identity, but the attributes of identity) to the advantages of exploitation.

A particular way of life is maintained in a particular frame. I propose to examine one such frame, drawing my material from the Debates of the House of Assembly of the Republic of South Africa between 1948 and 1968. During this period, the frame used by the National Party was relatively stable. The advantage of political debate to the student of paradigms is that political parties attempt to present an image of stability, though there may be turmoil behind the scenes. These paradigms are like the paradigms Kuhn found in science: the presentation of policy to the public is the political equivalent of the presentation of science to the student in school or first year at the university. All appears calm and calculable. All problems are soluble within the paradigm. If we accept this front, we may wonder how anything can ever change, how men can ever see beyond the paradigm.

Seeing beyond the party line is difficult, yet that does not mean that the party line is not disputed, out of the public view. Politicians, like the scientists who work within a paradigm, have no more than a family resemblance to each other. What they present is an unchanging policy which changes suddenly, in such a way that nothing has changed.

How is this possible? What is being presented is style, an image, a way of doing things. As Edelman remarks:

Every message is bound to have both semantic and esthetic content; but the analytic distinction leads to some non-obvious conclusions. (1971: 36)

Within a very broad semantic range, the aesthetic of the party must remain constant. The Conservative Party differs from the Labour Party and Democrats from Republicans rather in the way that Impressionists differ from Cubists. They have ways of doing what they do, rather than fixed policies.

Political presentation is concerned with what Boxer (1979) calls subject-referenced rather than object-referenced knowledge. We must get the feeling that we are dealing with the same people, doing things in the same manner; not necessarily doing the same things. A great show is made of dealing with issues, yet Mrs Thatcher's hairdo and friendliness are as important as what she says, within broad limits. What the voter wants is order and meaning; the difference between parties is as much aesthetic as substantial. Meaning is destroyed by information, the voter rejects or neglects information which he cannot assimilate to an aesthetic preference.

Moles (1968: 208) describes the tension between meaning and information in a set of contrasts:

Meaning	*Information*
order	disorder
predictable	unpredictable
banal	original
redundant	information
intelligible	novel
simple	complex

It is to preserve meaning that parties present a constant view of events, long after members have realized that his view is obsolete. A new picture must form before anything can be done.

A party can be attacked with information, but it will remain undamaged until its image is spoilt. This has to be done by discrediting its style. Issues have to be carefully chosen to accomplish this: they have to show that the style of the party is incompetent. A party of peace will be discredited by the failure of repeated concessions, as Chamberlain's was; or a party of law and order by the apprehension that it is too weak.

The frame of identities presented by a party is part of its aesthetic. It has to be held intact for a period, and when it changes it must change in such a way that it is aesthetically consistent with what went before. The National Party in South Africa faces this problem in changing the basis of its categorical system from racial differences to ethnic differences. Challengers from the left and the right do not find this credible. Their challenge takes the form of reference to characterizing statements which, it is said, show that there is no change at all. To profess change and be accused of not changing is as embarrassing as not changing when a new picture of the political scene is demanded by a majority of the electorate. The style and competence of the performance is called in question.

I turn now to the frame of identities as presented in the Debates.

The frame

The Debates refer to various categories of persons: races, occupations, nations, political parties and so forth. The range of possible social categories and roles is enormous. What is more interesting is the identities of the people who fall into the categories. This is the key question in human society. In any social vision, it is not merely roles, but the identities of those who play the roles, which is important. That is what we try to discover and control. In political vision, there is also a reference identity, in terms of which the system is organized. This mythical figure is the ideological pivot of the social enterprise; it is to preserve his well-being that the drama is undertaken. He symbolizes the position from which society is to be understood. In South Africa, the pivotal position is, for National Party members, the traditional Afrikaner, embodied in the Trekker, the Boer. Taking up this position and viewing the South African scene from it, we see that identity is divided into two planes: black and white. Now, within each of these planes, there are traditional and modern identities, and there are natural and estranged identities. As members of Parliament argue for particular courses of action, they reveal much more fully than they do in the finished Act how this structure of social identities determines policy. Members reveal constructs which may never be translated into Acts of Parliament because Acts require (a) the construction and selection of behaviour which can achieve the goals implied by unrealized systems of constructs; and (b) an appreciation of resources and consequences.

How can one extract constructs which are widely shared from the flow of debate? The method which I have chosen is to try to find *clear cases*. That is, I search for statements which seem to me to be typical and which are not contradicted by other members of the party. This is rather like the way in which linguists search for clear cases when constructing linguistic arguments, though there is a large pool of native speakers to whom they can readily appeal when exhibiting a clear case. What I would need, to make the parallel exact, is a team of investigators all thoroughly acquainted with the Debates of the House of Assembly to agree that the statements I have chosen are well-formed expressions of Nationalist Party construing, in the sense that they are *revealing* and that they are *widely shared*. This introduces a factor which is not generally part of linguistic argument: the frequency argument. Often, though, it is implicit. An appeal is made to *dialect*, or the pool of statements accepted in some community. In sociolinguistics, samples are taken which are judged to be well formed, often on the basis of the investigator's own observations, since, in the course of study, he becomes the person best qualified to observe. This is a common problem in any area where new observations are made. There is no difficulty, in principle, in getting other skilled observers. Training schools may be set up (e.g. psychoanalysts train people to observe the critical data, linguists train students to hear what they hear).

I shall now produce a corpus of statements which show common constructs about identities in South Africa. They are all made by members of the National Party. They are all embodied in speeches which strengthen my interpretations of the constructs. These speeches are too long and too numerous to be reproduced.

An alternative procedure would be to examine the construing of one person only, but it is my purpose to show here that these are not the constructs of one person but of a community of persons with a high degree of commonality in their construing of a particular area of social reality. What I shall now do is to provide

(a) a corpus of clear cases, or typical statements;
(b) a structure of identities based on this corpus; and
(c) a note on methodology.

The National Party was selected for analysis because it governs South Africa and its construction of identity has, therefore, an intrinsic interest for those attempting to understand South African affairs. In addition, its members exhibit a greater commonality in their construing than the members of other parties do. This is probably both a cause and a consequence of political success.

CLEAR CASES

(All references are to the Debates of the House of Assembly. The final numbers refer to columns. Asterisks indicate words inserted by me to indicate both denotation and connotation, as derived from the member's own speech.)

1 Native Representatives frequent 'the semi-civilized Native, who tries to appropriate the civilization of the European and who thereby does his people harm instead of helping to build them up by utilization of his knowledge.' 'The farmer has done more for the uplifting and civilizing of the Native in our country than all the foreign churches.' (J. V. L. Liebenberg, 1948: 1394–5)

2 'Give him [the Native]* what is his own and what he loves and build upon that in future, and if you do so you will create more satisfaction; if you are looking for a bulwark against communism, there is your bulwark against communism.' (D. F. Malan, 1948: 1430)

3 Apartheid 'will enable them [Natives]* at the same time to retain their national character.' (D. F. Malan, 1948: 218)

4 In the city there is 'an accumulation of unemployed Natives who are engaged solely in robbery and theft'. (J. G. W. van Niekerk, 1948: 1594)

5 'I may tell you that the leaders of the gangs of criminals, for instance on the Witwatersrand, are not people who come from the reserves. They are persons who have had a so-called education in the cities, who have received this kind of education, and the result is that they have become criminals. What is their value to their own people? The so-called educated Native is not worth anything to his people. His own people despise him; the white population looks down with contempt on him.' (M. D. C. de Wet Nel, 1948: 2428)

6 'It is not as if you were planting lily bulbs when you

devote large sums of money for their education. You are, I think, rather sowing dragon's teeth...' (D. J. Scholtz, 1948: 2440)

7   We must guard against 'crushing their national characteristics under a cloak of philanthropy'. (P. W. Botha, 1949: 5091)

8   'Natives on the farms are the most fortunate Natives in the whole country...we know their mentality and what is good for them. [City Natives]* imagine they are white people.' (A. Steyn, 1948: 1403)

9   'I have been right throughout Africa and if up in the north one calls a Swahili an African he will become a Mau Mau.' (G. H. F. Strydom, 1958: 799) And '...the word *African* today is merely a propaganda word which has come into use under communist influence.' (A. Jonker, 1958: 4021)

10 'If there is one reason why these honourable members [the Native Representatives]* should no longer be in this House, it is the fact that they are trying to entrench this word [African]* in the dictionaries of South Africa.' (H. E. Martins, 1958: 4070)

11 'We should assist the Native to develop according to his own nature and capabilities, and his own traditions, and we should assist him to develop through our guardianship.' (J. G. Strydom, 1958: 44)

12 'Native Sap...wants to become a white man...' (G. F. Froneman, 1958: 3842) (SAP refers to South African Party — the opposition party.)

13 'Once the detribalized and westernized Native returns for a while to his own country and his own people, he soon realizes what he really is.' (M. S. F. Grobler, 1958: 2432)

14 'But there is nothing dangerous in our affording every nation in South West Africa the right to get what they deserve, a right allocated to them by the Almighty to be a separate group, a separate nation, with a distinctive

goal, a distinctive identity, and with a distinctive ideal.' (G. F. Froneman, 1968: 5445)

15 Self-determination is an 'inherent, inborn right which was given to them [the Bantu people]* by their creator', and 'self-realization is the inalienable right of each and every nation.' (M. C. Botha, 1968: 5485)

16 'If the Native has a good mealie crop this year, he does not work for the next few years.' (J. J. Haywood, 1948: 1628)

17 'It is the task of the European to protect him [the Native]*...even against Europeans.' (M. D. C. de Wet Nel, 1948: 2922)

18 The Native 'is in many respects a weakling when he comes into conflict with the White man. I would not like to use the word "coward" but he is a weakling. He feels inferior to the White man and he will not lightly fight or oppose the White man without the support of another White man...The difficulty facing South Africa is that there are Whites who agitate amongst and incite the non-Whites. Such White people find support overseas and this strengthens the position of the agitator in this country and disturbs the good relations which should exist.' (M. S. F. Grobler, 1958: 2431)

19 'Most of the Natives who are paid £10 or £15 a month in this country do not really earn £5...I think that is a scandalous remark to make, to compare the white Senate with Natives...' (A. J. R. van Rhyn, 1958: 784)

20 'One of the worst crimes that we as Whites have committed against the Natives in South Africa is that we have spoonfed him.' (W. A. Maree, 1958: 3987)

21 'They [the Native Representatives]* quite unjustifiably expect each White man to carry four Natives to a higher standard of living.' (M. J. v. d. Berg, 1958: 3905)

22 'The Bantu will never be able to absorb the development we bring him with our know-how and capital in the same way as we were able to absorb development from

overseas in our country of whites as opposed to whites.' (P. R. de Jager, 1968: 1988)

23 'Surely the fact that you work for a man does not give you the right to run his affairs.' (J. B. Vorster, 1968: 4037)

24 '...we want to give them their own homelands, so that they need not always remain under our wing.' (P. R. de Jager, 1968: 1985)

25 'I do not expect my guest to play with my children in the nursery if I want to entertain him in my lounge... I do not expect my guest to associate with my servant in the servants' room.' (G. F. Froneman, 1968: 6301) (The speaker is referring to the question of whether foreign African diplomats should be treated as whites or as Bantu.)

26 '...if it does happen in future that the Europeans can do without the services of the Natives, the ideal of total apartheid which is preached in some circles, may become practical politics.' (Dr E. G. Jansen, 1950: 4711)

27 'The Apartheid policy was described as that which was practicable in the direction of what one looked upon as ideal. Nobody will deny that, for the Natives as well as for the Europeans, total separation would have been the ideal if that had been the course of history.' (Dr H. F. Verwoerd, 1952: 7858)

28 Those who use the term 'African' 'want to impress the world that Africa is not the home of the White man or of other peoples' and 'they want to hurt the Afrikaners. They know that the English word African can only be translated, if it has to be translated, by something like "Afrikane" – only the "r" of "Afrikaner" falls away.' (Dr H. F. Verwoerd, 1958: 4052)

29 'Not only did they burn her, they ate parts of her body. Most natives will cut your throat like a sheep and they will not even feel sorry.' (G. H. F. Strydom, 1958: 801)

30 'As long as agitators incite them [the Natives]* and as

long as they are represented in this House by these Native Representatives and as long as these representatives speak as they have today, the Natives will never be satisfied.' (M. S. F. Grobler, 1958: 3850)

31 Separate Development: 'A policy which does not mean that the white man is superior towards other people in this country, but that all the population groups differ from one another.' (N. C. van R. Sadie, 1958: 158)

32 'If our policy ends in total territorial apartheid, not the slightest objection will be raised to it from this side of the House.' (B. Coetzee, 1968: 3797)

33 'If the Bantu is not doing anything here he may just as well go and stay there [in the homelands]*. We resettle many elderly people... There are many Bantu children here who do nothing. They simply stay with their mother or with their grandmother or whoever it may be. They do not work at all. Then they may just as well go and stay in their homelands and do nothing.' (G. F. Froneman, 1968: 90)

34 'The Bantu are here to sell their labour in the white homeland and if the Bantu do not want to sell their labour here, why should they be here?' (A. H. Vosloo, 1968: 6620)

35 'The hon. member [Mrs Suzman]* must not think that we have forgotten that she said as long ago as 1961 that a single black face in this House would improve its appearance a great deal.' (B. Pienaar, 1968: 2254)

36 '...her people [Mrs Suzman's]* exploited the black man.' (A. L. Raubenheimer, 1968: 3412)

37 'They [the Bantu]* will be used as voting cattle.' (P. C. Roux, 1968: 5260)

38 'According to my reading of the signs of the times, the public will insist within a period of ten years that a criminal charge be brought against any person in South Africa who dares to advocate anything in conflict

with the maintenance of the colour bar.' (M. J. van den Berg, 1968: 148)

A STRUCTURE OF IDENTITIES

When we examine the data we find the following constructs occurring frequently.

Adult-child (construct of white superiority). It is clear that black and white planes of social identity are separate from statements 2, 3, 6, 7, 11, 12, 15, 16, 17, 19, 22, 24, 26, 27, 28, 29, 32, 33, 34, 35, 38. This separation often has a particular content, in which whites are construed as adult relatives to childish blacks, or, more benevolently, as guardians of blacks. See statements 1, 8, 11, 16, 17, 18, 19, 20, 21, 22, 23, 24, 25, 29, 36, 37.

Traditional-modern (construct of modernization). This construct is rather commonplace and we have taken only a few statements to show it: 1, 4, 5, 6, 7, 8, 13.

Estranged-natural (construct of estrangement). This refers to estrangement from one's own people and attempts to imitate those of a different group — imitation whites, agitators, *kaffir-boeties* ('nigger-lovers'). 1, 2, 3, 4, 5, 7, 9, 10, 11, 12, 13, 14, 15, 17, 30, 31.

Note that:
(i) Several statements exhibit a combination of constructs.
(ii) This list concentrates on the black plane.
(iii) These statements all have a negatively evaluated and a positively evaluated pole; furthermore, they form a system (which I shall attempt to construct) and this system shows among other things, how various identities are evaluated.
(iv) these statements were made between 1948 and 1968; since then, the most important change is that it is not so widely believed that blacks are inferior.

A spatial metaphor may help us to understand the system of constructs used to determine identity. This metaphor represents the perspective of members of the National Party.

Figure 1. Structure of identities from the perspective of the National Party, up to 1968

(a) The system of constructs and the evaluations attached to them

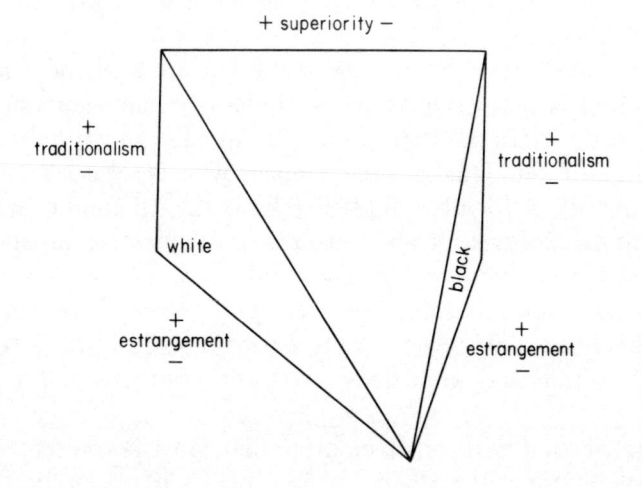

+ superiority −

+ traditionalism −   + traditionalism −

white   black

+ estrangement −   + estrangement −

(b) The system of constructs with the reference and complementary identities inserted

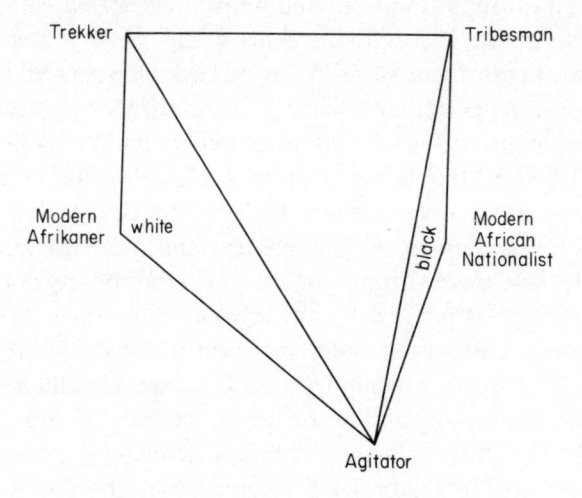

Trekker   Tribesman

Modern Afrikaner   white   Modern African Nationalist   black

Agitator

The spatial metaphor may take many forms; the criterion used here is simply that the information should be presented clearly. It is important to realize that this is an illustration, not a geometrical figure of which the sides are vectors. The acuteness or obtuseness of the angles has no quantitative significance.

The main features of the metaphor have already been presented in discussing the view of identity that is commonly held in the National Party. First, it must locate the reference identity of the Trekker, the Pioneer who is regarded as the founder of Afrikaner identity relative to its contemporary identities. Politics, when we take its expressive aspect, is conducted to maintain a reference identity and the system of identities that this reference identity implies. If we wish to understand a person, we have to understand him by reference to what he is and what he is not, to the contrasts that define him.

The second feature of identity that must be presented in the metaphor is that there are two planes of social identity. All other distinctions are made within each of these planes. The distinctions are made in terms of the contrasts adult/childish; traditional/modern; and natural/estranged.

To whom do these distinctions apply? Every system of identities, taken from some point of view, consists of a reference identity (exemplary when it is admired by those who take that point of view) and complementary identities. The system of identities is made up of those who play a part in the story (or history) of the reference identity. In this case, the reference identity is exemplary; the Voortrekkers are admired, they are celebrated in many ceremomies by representatives of the National Party; the Afrikaner nation — of which the National Party is the principal political instrument — has construed its history around the history and character of the Trekkers; the principal dates of South African history are the dates of the Great Trek, and subsequent history is seen as an achievement or a failure to the degree that the implications of their search for independence are achieved or not achieved. Such great events as the Day of the Covenant, the First and Second Boer Wars, the Recognition of Afrikaans as an Official Language in South Africa, and the coming of the Republic, fulfil their destiny. In this history, who are the others? There are various levels of detail at which this could be investigated. One might examine all references to others — and the list could be quite long — as they are found in textbooks and in orations and in the historical examples of the National Party members.

A more general schema is possible — one which develops out of the contrasts of superiority, estrangement and modernization. This general schema refers to certain rather abstract identities which can act as containers for more definite ones. It is a general schema which contains the identities of all those who have supported or threatened Afrikaner identity. The names may have changed, but the general identities have remained constant.

If we examine the *white plane* first, the achievement of Afrikaner identity has been threatened by those who are *modern* and those who are *estranged*. We may lump the two together for certain purposes and speak of all those who are *spoiled* (to borrow a term from Goffman). Spoiled identities are urbanized, modern people who do not respect the values of the Trekker. Those who are most spoiled are those who are not merely modern but estranged. On the *white plane*, the complementary identities construed in this way are, ranging from the least spoiled to the most spoi[1] d:-

    The Nationalist Afrikaner, who is proud of Afrikaner tradition.

    Urbanized Afrikaners who are losing traditions.

    Agitators, meddling priests, communists, and other who do not respect the traditional distinction between white and black. This is the most estranged position.

The *black plane* is the mirror image of the *white plane*. When one refers to speeches by Nationalist leaders, there is always a high degree of respect (though patronising) for the traditional Tribal Man. He is the counterpart of the Trekker. He is the figure who complements the story of the Trekker. There is the added advantage that the superiority of the Trekker has already been proved by conquest, so that traditional blacks do not threaten traditional Afrikaner identity. One might say that the Tribal Man is a necessary ingredient of that identity, since without him there would not have been any glorious history. But, from the National Party point of view, the *spoiled* black is a different matter. He is urbanized and estranged from traditional ways. Again, one can arrange complementary identities from the least to the most spoiled:-

Black Nationalists (who accept Separate Development).

Black Nationalists (whose aim is a common polity).

Agitators, communists and others who do not respect traditional distinctions between white and black.

In both planes, two identities are clear: they represent a crystallisation of identity and of the possible choices. They represent revolutionary alternatives. The two identity contrasts are:

Traditional: Trekker/Tribesman

Estranged: Agitator/Agitator

Translated into modern terms the first opposition becomes:

White Nationalist/Black Nationalist

The second opposition remains the same. 'Agitators' are various: they may be liberals, priests or communists. They are smitten by the same law: the Suppression of Communism Act, or, since 1976, by the Internal Security Act. This is easily understood in terms of the structure of identities.

The basic point here is that identity is defined in terms of admission to social positions. The first broad distinction (black/white) is a distinction between those who are admitted and those who are not. The supplementary identities are those who challenge or support this broad position.

One might comment on the relation between identity and Marx's concept of class.

If we take it that Marx was most concerned with a social identity which was based on private ownership of the means of production, then his theory is a special theory. If private ownership disappears, does class disappear?

On the other hand, if we take social identity to be based on access to social positions, then class differences – based on control of access to these positions – will exist whether private ownership continues or not. The social class of men of a given identity will then be determined by whether they are eligible or not eligible to controlling positions in an imperatively coordinated system, which is an institution in which there are relations of authority. Men of different social identities will belong to the same class if they are equally eligible to positions of power. Dahrendorf has put the matter rather well:

...if private property disappears (empirical hypotheses), then there are no longer classes (trick of definition). If there are no longer any classes, there is no alienation (speculative postulate). The realm of liberty is realised on earth (philosophical idea). Had Marx, conversely, defined property by authority relations, his empirical observations would not have 'fitted', and he would have had to drop his philosophy of history. For effective private property may disappear empirically, but authority relations can do so only by the magic trick of the system maniac. (1959: 30–1)

Thus, to be absolutely clear about it, in any given society there is a relation between social identity and access to social positions. The right of access to positions of power is class position and the same class position may be held by persons of different identities. Identity, or the relation between identity and position or the existing system of positions, will be disputed when the class position of men of a given identity is unfavourable.

The identities in the structure which represents the National Party's point of view are the identities of those who are contesting access to positions of power. The opposition of Nationalists (black and white) would not upset the identities of the participants, though it might upset their relations to positions of power. The opposition of Nationalists and Agitators is an opposition which threatens both identity — since Agitators challenge the distinction between black and white — and access to the positions of power — since they support a political system which could end the Afrikaner majority by allowing blacks to enter Parliament.

From what we have said it is also clear that the contrasts are evaluative contrasts. That is, where *traditional* is contrasted with *modern*, it is usually to the disadvantage of what is modern. Where *natural* is contrasted with *estranged*, this is even more strongly the case. The terms *adult/childish* show quite clearly that the persons to whom they attach are positively and negatively evaluated.

When we examine the figures — the reference and the complementary identities — we see this even more clearly.

Evaluations. The poles of the construct system are evaluative. Or, to put it another way, the polar identities at the intersects of the constructs are positively or negatively evaluated. Thus, the reference identity of Trekker is most highly valued, the negative identity of spoiled white or black is least valued.

If we start with the distinction between black and white, it will come as no surprise that white is more highly valued than black.

This is shown in statements 18 (weakling); 19 (overpaid); 20 (spoonfed); 21 (have to be carried); 22 (cannot absorb development); 29 (will cut your throat); and 37 (voting cattle).

When we refer to spoiled blacks (modern, estranged blacks), we find the following judgements: 1 (semi-civilized); 4 (city robbers); 5 (so-called educated); 6 (dragon's teeth); 8 (imagine they are white); 12 (wants to become a white man); 33 (superfluous); 34 (labour units). This negative evaluation of blacks is demonstrated in actions as well as words. I shall illustrate this simply by reference to the fate of 'surplus' blacks in the cities. Blacks who are unable to meet the qualifying conditions of Section 10 of the Natives' (Urban Areas) Consolidation Act, 1945, as amended, or are considered as being 'idle or undesirable' under Section 29 of Act 42 of 1964, are expelled from the towns. 'It was reported in the House of Assembly that in 1968, 61,658 Africans who were not economically active were removed from white areas. Mr G. F. van L. Froneman said in March 1969 that there were 3,807,465 Africans in white urban areas who in his opinion were "superfluous", they were dependents of bread-winners' (Desmond [n. d.]: 14). Furthermore, in the period 1967–8 there were 693,661 prosecutions for pass law offences, an average of 1,900 per day (ibid.: 13). Ellis (1974) has demonstrated an exponential growth of the number of pass law prosecutions per year.

It is pretty clear that people who are treated in this way are regarded as useless objects and not as people. They must produce wealth and then disappear.

Tribal blacks are more acceptable than spoiled blacks. This is illustrated in statements 2 (bulwark against communism); 3 (national character); 8 (farm Native); 9 (Swahili, not African); 11 (own nature); 13 (power of tradition); 14 (Not dangerous); 15 (inalienable rights).

I shall now examine the way in which spoiled whites (modern, estranged) are construed by members of the National Party. A full demonology would reveal that spoiled whites wish to undermine the Afrikaner. That is one of their first aims: it is a conviction which grows out of the history of South Africa, a history in which the Trekkers searched for the place where they could be left alone, to live their own kind of life, and in which they were pursued by the British until the Transvaal and Free State Republics were extinguished. There is now a Republic of South Africa: will it also disappear? In the list of statements above, particular attention is drawn to 1 (foreign churches compared to farmer);

98 IDENTITY TRAPS

Figure 2 Exponential growth of the number of pass law prosecutions per year (thousands of individuals). (From Ellis, 1974 – based on figures supplied by F. Wilson)

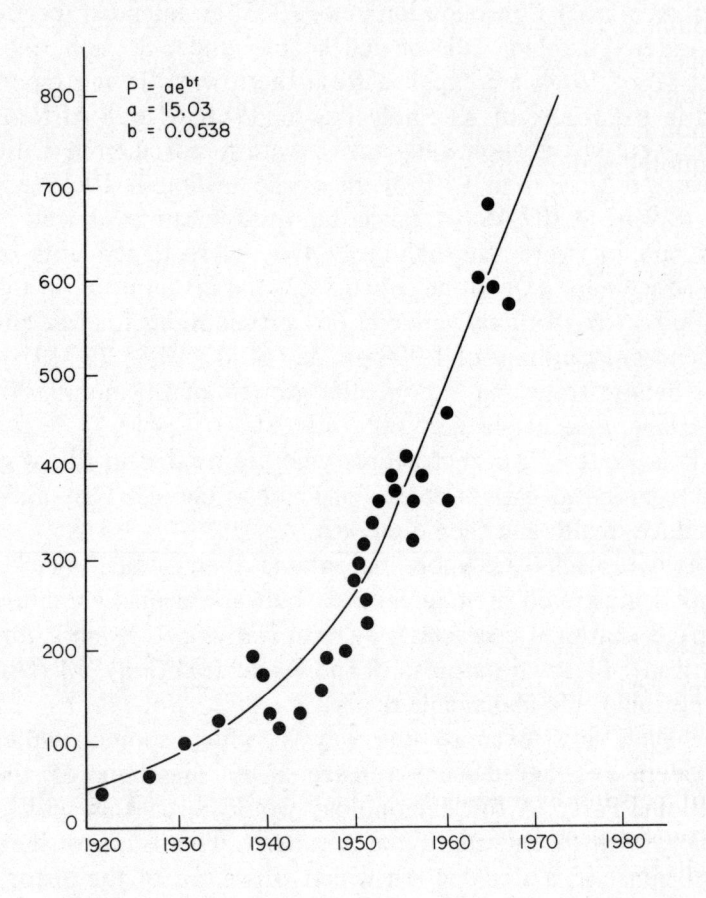

$P = ae^{bf}$
$a = 15.03$
$b = 0.0538$

7 (foreign churchmen besmirch original European population); 10 (Native Representatives agitate); 21 (Native Representatives expect the unreasonable); 30 (Agitators prevent Natives from being satisfied); 35 and 36 (Mrs Suzman and her people).

On the other hand, it is the farmer, who is the traditional and true white, who civilizes the Native, as we can see from statements 1, 7 and 8.

Summary: characteristics of the data. The thirty-eight statements quoted above were produced by twenty-six speakers, fourteen of whom achieved cabinet status, though they were not necessarily members of the cabinet when making the quoted statements.

Table 1: *Classification of statements*

Year of Statement	Cabinet	Speaker's Status Non-cabinet	Total
1948	4	6	10
1958	6	7	13
1968	7	5	12
other	3	0	3
Total	20	18	13

A NOTE ON METHODOLOGY

The first question which could be asked is whether the statements are so representative that any characterization of them would be an *exhaustive* characterization and categorization of persons by members of the National Party. *No claim is made that this is so.* It is difficult to see how an exhaustive characterization of the categories used by all speakers in a very large party could be achieved.

A second, more interesting, question is whether the picture is widely shared in the National Party. In order to see whether this is so, it is more useful to look for negative instances than to extend the list of positive instances.

That is, we don't ask whether the list could be extended to include more positive instances — it could be, by hundreds of statements – but whether there are instances in which Nationalist speakers have spoken of urbanized Africans as *natural* and tribal Africans as *spoiled*; whether Nationalist speakers have spoken of Africans as *adult* and responsible rather than *childish* and irresponsible relative to whites; and whether Nationalist speakers have spoken of Africans as belonging to the same plane as whites. I suggest, on the basis of a close scrutiny of debates in the years 1948, 1958 and 1968, that such negative instances are rare and atypical. Failure to find such negative instances may reflect blindness or bias on the part of the investigator, but their infrequency, as opposed to the high frequency of positive instances, is sufficient evidence for the representativeness of the former. A second way of asking the same question is to ascertain whether a speaker who produces a statement revealing the assumption that Africans are childish, or that black and white are irreconcilably different in some deep and mysterious way, produces reaction within his own party. If there is no reaction, then he is likely to be voicing a common assumption. The lack of reaction, and the repetition of these assumptions in debate after debate by debater after debater, leads us to conclude that they are widely shared.

Government policy has been constrained by the narrow identity frame of the National Party. This is one of the grave consequences of what was called an identity squeeze in the previous chapter.

Is there any way out, starting from the present system?

Possible developments in the identity frame

Over the last ten years (1968–78) the National Party has attempted to change one of the characterizations of its identity frame – the political superiority of whites relative to blacks – by substituting the category 'nation' for that of 'race'. Nation is linked to ethnicity, and permits political distinctions within the black group, such as Xhosa, Venda, Tswana, etc.

There is a major difficulty in this attempt. The distinction, embodied in law and practice, between those who may intermarry and those who may not, between those who must carry passes and those who move freely within the Republic, and between those who qualify to vote and stand in elections to the House of Assembly of the Republic and those who may not, is a distinction between black and white, not a distinction between nations based on ethnicity.

A careful examination of policy since 1948 shows remarkable stability rather than remarkable change. Immediately after he had come to power in 1948 at the head of the National Party, Prime Minister Malan stated the positive side of the policy of apartheid in terms which are almost identical with statements of the positive side of separate development. The purpose was 'to call into being institutions for them (blacks) in their own reserves, and to promote and further develop institutions of their own which will enable them to have a large measure of self-government and which will enable them at the same time to retain their own national character' (1948: 214). If whites are not to have any say in the reserves why should natives have any say in the white areas (1948: 219)?

The consequence of this view is still to be found in the policy of linking citizenship to the 'homelands'. Even though we shall continue to need black workers, 'the fact that you work for a man does not give you the right to run his affairs' (Vorster, 1968: 4037).

A crucial test of the theory of separate development is the position it gives the coloured people of South Africa — a population of two and a half million people (out of a total of nearly twenty-five million) of mixed descent. They are Westernized, speak Afrikaans and English, and live almost entirely in 'white' areas of the Republic. There are no ethnic grounds for excluding them from the common polity; the grounds must be racial. The identity frame of the National Party (shared by the majority of whites) has not permitted their political integration.

Consider the following debate, in which the prime minister, Mr Vorster, is rebuking a member of the opposition for suggesting that the coloured people, many of whom are Afrikaans-speaking, should be regarded as Afrikaners.

> In other words, if any other group, for example Indians, should decide tomorrow that they will speak Afrikaans and become Protestants, then they will come and sit here?...If Bantu communities adopt Afrikaans as a language, and most of them are Christians too, then surely they too can come and sit here. Surely one is not bluffing anyone with stupid arguments of that kind. (Debates, 1968: 71)

(In the next section I shall mention some constitutional proposals to solve the problems of their political status.)

Categorizing people by nationality is a development which occurs largely *within* the framework of separation of white and black; yet to change an identity frame it is even more essential to change characterizations than to change categories.

What the critics of separate or plural development point to is that the substitution of *nation* for *race* is an attempt to introduce more acceptable categories while retaining the implications of being white or black.

There is, though, one definite change in characterization: the superiority of whites is no longer official doctrine. Inequality persists, but it has lost its theoretical support. It now persists as a matter of political practice, leaving open the possibility of change. Effective policy has to replace biology in maintaining the position of whites. This was always the case, one might say, but the assumptions are different.

What sorts of change are possible, given the perspectives of the different parties? Every dispensation must serve the interests of one or more political agents. The question we have to ask concerning any proposal, is: who will support it?

The serious alternatives are nationalism (in a framework of plural development) and Marxism.

Nationalism appeals to ethnic differences. A nationalist solution will be supported by most whites and possibly by some leaders of newly independent states. The appeal of this solution to whites is that it maintains differences in wealth and real power, but this is also its fatal weakness, and black leaders who settle for it would be settling for inferiority. This policy, as it stands, opens backward into history – it attempts to recreate a past in which tribes existed as independent political powers. To meet the future, it would have to acknowledge the claims of industrial workers, who cannot possibly belong to any tribal region.

Marxism appeals to the class interests of the relatively impoverished and politically excluded black workers. This is the rapidly growing and dynamic section of South African society. Its strength is that the main social fractures of race, exclusion from power, and economic class, are almost superimposed. Where an important identity marker such as race coincides with class divisions, we have the basis for intransigent class conflict. The weakness of the Marxist solution lies in the fact that it ignores ethnic differences (language and tribal affiliations – and here I include the tribal affiliations of the whites, which are extremely deep).

What is needed is an impossible project, which will take both class and ethnic differences into account. The objection to a Marxist solution (where ethnic differences are considerable) is its excessive centralization of power in the state, leading to the domination of all by those in power. Minority groups are not protected. The fundamental objection to pluralism, as conceived by the National Party, is that the poor and powerless remain poor and powerless.

The impossible project which would lead to a solution of these problems is the development of socialist pluralism, in which authority would be decentralized and wealth would be distributed. It is not easy to see what political agency would support such a move. What will almost certainly happen, therefore, is a struggle between white interests expressed as a policy of plural development and black interests expressed in Marxist language.

Yet to say this is not to predict the worst – irreconcilable and bloody conflict. Struggle between interested parties is the essence of even the most peaceful politics. Two sides which start out from irreconcilable positions find themselves, as often as not, in a situation no one has anticipated. Politics is not mechanical: there is the human factor. Mugabe and Machel attempt to make room in their Marxist programmes for the encouragement of private enterprise.

The con

The modification of identity frame which led to the creation of independent states such as the Transkei, BophutaTswana and Venda created the problem of recognizing the 'nationhood' of the coloured and Indian people.

I wish to investigate the way in which members of the Coloured Persons' Representative Council (CRC) experience their 'national' identity.

The first thing to be said about the CRC is that it has failed. It has been dissolved. It was constituted in 1964 as an advisory body, with limited legislative powers in the fields of finance, local government, education, community welfare, pensions and coloured rural settlements. No bill may be introduced without the approval of the minister of Coloured Affairs, and all bills require the State President's consent. There are twenty nominated and forty elected members, a fact that enabled the pro-government Federal Party to hold office in the first years of the CRC in spite of the fact that the party had lost the elections.

There is a similar arrangement for Indians, who are represented by the SA Indian Council. A constitutional committee was set up in 1980 to investigate possible constitutions for the future.

A con, as I have said already, is an attempt to manoeuvre others into supporting our frame, though it gives them an inferior position. Needless to say, cons may be more or less successful. Where they are less successful, those who are conned are uneasy and may, under favourable conditions, express their unease. The process of 'identity resolution' (Breakwell, 1978) is set in train, resolving incompatibility by changing the internal criteria of identity (personal beliefs and knowledge) or the external criteria ('objective' norms and standards).

What a con attempts to achieve is resolution of incompatibility by the adaptation of internal criteria to external criteria imposed by the party attempting the con. The binding nature of frames of experience is well known from the work of Zimbardo (1975) on simulated prisons, Milgram (1974) on obedience, and Asch (1956) on conformity. And the nature of the activity in the CRC (salaries, the commitment to represent an electorate which has no voice, the 'only chance') is such that the participants are under great pressure to adjust their internal criteria to the external criteria imposed by the party. However, the process occurs also in a larger context. In 1976 there were riots in Soweto and other black centres, and blacks were joined by coloured youth. There is also the pressure on white South Africa from the external world. Thus, there is support for those who see the best resolution as adapting external rather than internal criteria. This starts a process of negotiation in which more has to be conceded to keep participants at the negotiating table — and here we see how the process of identity resolution can contribute to the breaking of ideology, under particular circumstances.

A complete con would be one in which identity resolution occurred by modifying internal criteria only, making them conform to external criteria. Indeed, the external criteria become the internal criteria, as Fanon and Mannoni showed, when a dominant group has overwhelming control of the symbols of power and status. But where there are unfavourable comparisons to be drawn, where there is a growing loss of control, the con is not likely to succeed. The coloured people are aware of the growth of black power and the fact that the white regime is under threat. The support for a positive re-evaluation of black identity is international; there are also many of the support factors of ethnic vitality described by Giles, Bourhis and Taylor (1977) for a strong black identity in South Africa.

The coloured group does not have the numbers or the independent language and culture to develop a politically successful identity of its own. Therefore we observe both denials of the political relevance of separate identities and attempts to align themselves with one or other powerful collective. In a count of speakers in the CRC who referred explicitly to identity in the debates over two years (1975 and 1976) I found the following:

Table 2: *Identity claims by speakers in the Coloured Persons' Representative Council*

Identity	Number of Speakers
Coloured	4
Black	5
Common	7
Reject coloured	2
Reject white	5

One can see, from the scatter of identifications, that representatives were not certain what identity to claim. Recent moves (rejection of the President's Council if blacks are not included) indicate a resolution of identity in favour of 'blackness'. It will be interesting to see how far this goes, in view of language and cultural differences.

In studying the Debates of the CRC there is no particular interest in picking out the contributions of those who support the government identity frame, often with slight reservations. Many of them are nominated members of the CRC. The fact is that the pro-government Federal Party gained fewer elected members than the anti-government Labour Party from the first election, and by 1975 the Labour Party was in power in spite of the twenty nominated members (in a Council of sixty) by which the government strengthened the Federal Party. The Labour Party returned thirty-one elected members to the eight of the Federal Party in 1975. Even more revealing, is the way in which the coloured electorate rejected the system: in 1969, thirty-seven per cent of the estimated qualified voters actually voted; in 1975, twenty-eight per cent of the estimated qualified voters voted.

Statements supporting the government identity frames are of the following kind (asterisks indicate that the statements have been translated from the Afrikaans):

1 'They [the government] are honouring and upholding the policy of separate development, and that is why we are here.' (Africa, 1975: 90)
2 'It is a fact that the Labour Party repeatedly pleaded the case of the Black man in this Council...but I often said to them, Mantanzima and Buthelezi have their own groups, they are leaders of their own people, yet the Labour Party persisted. They emphasized that they had taken the interests of the Black man to heart.'* (Swartz, 1975: 36)
3 'Nationalism, or Brown identity, is in touch with separateness, with differentiation, with individualism, with originality, with otherness.'* (Bergins, 1975: 186)

What is of greater interest in estimating the success of the con are attempts to break frame. In the previous chapter, I said that some cons require a theoretical stance for their detection, whereas others can be detected by the unease of the conned and by their attempts to break frame by proposing alternatives.

The unease of the members of the CRC has been expressed in Labour Party boycotts of the opening of the CRC in 1977 and 1978, in attempts to prevent approval of the budget since 1975, in motions to abolish the CRC, in frequent comments on the act of participation, and in ridicule. Finally, all parties have requested the abolition of the Council.

Examples of the use of self-ridicule in showing up the frame are given below:

4   'Everything else, Bill, you gave away because your Lord and master said: "Hotnot, you will carry out my orders."* (Adams, 1975: 61)
5   'Ja baas' repeatedly. (1975: 113, 117, 128)
6   'Who is talking in the kitchen?' (Africa, 1975: 173)
7   'You are a Hotnot and you are a Griekwa...You are still living in the era of the Great Trek, Hotnot.' (Adams, 1975: 192)
8   'You may look like a Hotnot, but you are a human being.' (Muller, 1975: 223)

The position of participants in the Council is diagnosed in these sharp comments: they are reinforcing their own position of inferiority by accepting the CRC.

A variety of alternative frames are proposed by members attempting to use the platform provided by the CRC.

9   'What is the citizenship right of a Coloured? Why does he ask for Coloured citizenship? Why does he not ask for universal suffrage?' (Adams, 1975: 61)
10 '...strive to do away with all forms of apartheid, whether parallel or whatever it may be called, I call it ungodly.'* (Muller, 1975: 72)
11 'Why is the White man now making these verligte noises? ..We, the Black elite, must now be absorbed into the White elite so that we can become the co-oppressors of the poor...' (Curry, 1975: 30)
12 'We condemn in total...separate development, and I would request, in support of the hon. Mr Africa's

recommendation, the Opposition and the Independents to withdraw now and I give you my assurance that we will walk out with you.' (Leon, 1975: 168)

13 'I have said it here: I hate the term "Coloured", I hate the term "Brown person", I am a South African citizen:'* (Jacobs, 1975: 218)

14 'I must state without fear of contradiction that Brown domination, Black domination, White domination must be opposed equally, must be eradicated.'* (Rabie, 1975: 248)

15 'But we should not have any tag in South Africa. We should be prepared to be South Africans.' (Nash, 1976: 71)

16 Bergins 'shows his and his party's commitment to government by prescription, and that for a section only of the Black oppressed when he calls the Coloured people, and this despite the fact that this very section has demonstrated in these last few months that their destiny is completely bound up with that of all the oppressed people of this country.' (Ebrahim, 1976: 125)

17 'We are South Africans and I don't see myself as anything else, only as a South African.' (Boezak, 1976: 146)

18 '...why should we depart from the Westminster system of government? In the British Constitution we have democracy enshrined.' (Reed, 1975: 187)

19 'Mr Chairman, the honourable member has mentioned Black consciousness and also Coloured consciousness. Would the honourable member agree with me when I say that both have been brought about by White power and White consciousness?'*... 'Yes, I concede that, but I would prefer us not to have White consciousness, Black or Brown consciousness – let us be mankind conscious.'* (Jacobs, 1976: 216)

It is clear from all this that the majority – even of those who attempt to participate in the government's plans by getting elected to the CRC – cannot accept the identity frame that is offered them by the government. Yet what can we say of the alternatives presented and of the hope for a common South African citizenship and a Westminster-type democracy?

Perhaps we have to say what Malraux said to de Gaulle in 1945, speaking of the options before France at the time.

Liberalism is a sentiment; not a political programme — a sentiment that can exist in several parties, but cannot create one. (Malraux, 1970: 99)

That is certainly true of South Africa in 1980. The task of liberalism is to restore the human scale to mass movements — to nationalism and communism. The claims of the individual must be continually inserted into the claims of the masses. Liberalism is often dismissed with contempt because ordinary liberals despair of gaining support for a programme without any popular foundation. When the choice is between powerful, self-interested movements, any attempt to make a programme of liberalism is often a mistake. What is necessary is that those who align themselves with one or the other movement should be reminded of the liberal spirit, of ways in which the harsh outlines of their programmes can allow freedom of choice to individuals. It is the function of liberalism to assert variety and the limitations of power.

5
Images

In this chapter I shall attempt to do two things. Firstly, I shall show the relation between issues, images, situations and policies. Secondly, I shall discuss the way in which our construal of situations limits the directions we can go in politics. The theoretical support for this discussion will be largely from Kelly's (1955) theory of personal constructs and the material used will be drawn from South African politics. However, the focus of attention is neither personal construct theory nor South African politics. What is intended is a discussion of political processes.

Images and incidents

In politics we work with idealized pictures of relations between people which can be called *images*. In an image, there are proper relations between classes of people which we prefer not to have disturbed by information to the contrary (Edelman, 1971). However, the world has a way of breaking in.

A *situation* is a match between an incident and an image. When there is a mismatch, we are faced with a political issue or even a crisis situation. A crisis threatens redefinition of our image; an issue can possibly be contained within our image. A crisis requires accommodation, an issue might be dealt with by assimilation, thus ensuring the stability of political life and the preservation of meaning and order.

When such a difference between an incident and an image enters the political consciousness of a collective agent such as a nation or a party, a policy must be devised to reconcile the two, if this is at all possible. Policy may mystify as well as cope realistically. A mystification is often achieved by a change of terms which leaves the real situation untouched.

Images are abstract schemas of public events to which incidents are assimilated. Many images start their lives quite innocent of politics, until particular events take certain of their features 'out of brackets'.

Politics flares up about incidents which disturb our images of public life.

Here are some examples. The images in the first list are simplified schemas of what we take for granted (in a particular context). Incidents bring the bracketed elements of the image to the foreground. Policy makers then have to decide what to do.

Images:
Food is produced on (privately owned) farms.
Jobs are open to (qualified) persons.
Plays are performed in (racially segregated) theatres.

The bracketed elements are taken out of brackets by critical incidents, such as the following:
Incidents:
Food is destroyed to maintain prices.
Women with children to care for are barred from jobs.
A black playwright is not allowed to attend a performance of his own play in a 'white' theatre.

Every image, no matter how often discussed, has many bracketed features, features which have been taken for granted because they have never been questioned by anyone. Critical situations arise when a mismatch is pointed out by some political agent, viewing the world from some perspective. Garfinkeling (1967) is the rule in politics. The bracketed elements are taken out like dirty linen and waved about to embarrass political opponents.

It should, by now, be clear that *image is ideology* adapted to political uses, to the discussion of problems in political life.

A clear definition of some of the elements of images will help us to understand how they work. Each image has, as one component, an identity frame, which we can represent by F. This identity frame is located in particular episodes — elements of social reality (Harré and Secord, 1972) — which we can represent by E.

An image is the relation F (E). It is an episode as enacted by persons in a particular identity frame. The image concerns the proper mode of enacting that episode and the proper characteristics and categories of actors. One might say that all this is contained in the separate concepts, F and E, but it is better to take these elements out of brackets, to bring them to the fore, and allow E to stand for the relations between the persons in F — the kinds of behaviour found in particular contexts, given particular classes of actors.

Then, given an identity frame (let us say, parents and their children) and a particular episode (a picnic; doing homework), we may expect certain things of them in a given culture. The occasion for saying anything about our expectation arises out of incidents during the enactment of the episode which bring aspects of the relationship to the foreground. A child refuses to do his homework when told to do it; parents spoil the picnic by insisting on everyone doing what parents find interesting.

An incident, then, is tested against an image and the result is a construal which we call a situation. If the match is satisfactory, nothing further may be required. If it is not, adjustments to the image or the incident may follow. The children may be spanked, or they may run away from their parents and refuse to go on picnics with them.

It follows from this conception of situations that the identity frame may change or the episode may be modified in order to adjust the image. Here is an example of an attempt to adjust an image by altering categories in the identity frame, taken from a debate on the naming of blacks in a white parliament. It is clearly seen, by the debaters, that adjustments of categories are usually accompanied by adjustments of characteristics.

The debate took place in 1958. The question at the time was whether people should be named (without consulting them) Bantu, Africans or Natives.

P. A. Moore, of the United Party, put the matter in terms of intelligibility:

We who speak English as our language try to speak English as are [sic] the English-speaking people in the rest of the world, and throughout the English-speaking world today. 'African' is the word used to describe the people who are called here 'Natives'. (Debates, 1958: 4077)

Dr Verwoerd, then Prime Minister, went on to pinpoint one of the political problems which change of name produced. He alleged that those who want to use the term 'African' for Black Africans.

...want to impress the world that Africa is not the home of the White man or of other peoples,...they want to hurt the Afrikaners. They know that the English word African can only be translated, if it has to be translated, by something like 'Afrikane. – only the 'r' of 'Afrikaner' falls away. (Debates, 1958: 4052)

There must be no confusion of African and Afrikaner. The two must be kept distinct because the political system is designed to preserve the distinctness of the Afrikaner and to achieve further distinctions between him and other groups.

H. E. Martins, of the National Party, expresses his indignation:

If there is one reason why these honourable members (the Native Representatives) should no longer be in this House, it is the fact that they are trying to entrench this word in the dictionaries of South Africa. (Debates, 1958: 4070)

Names have a great power to transform people and issues. If people are allowed to choose their own name — and not even the United Party pressed for this, though Mr Hughes suggested that it would be courteous — they might wish to choose other things too. While they can be named without considering their preferences, they need not be taken seriously.

G. H. F. Strydom of the National Party refers to the power of names:

I have been right throughout Africa and if up in the North one calls a Swahili an African he will become a Mau Mau. (Debates, 1958: 799)

The importance of names and modes of address as signals of status is well documented by Roger Brown (1965: 51-100). What Brown discusses on the level of theory is well understood by politicians on the level of practice.

An image can also be adjusted to an episode — or, to state the reverse, an image can be maintained by altering an episode to fit the image.

As an example of this I shall cite a debate on the feeding of black schoolchildren by government grant. The debate took place in 1948 and 1949, and much has occurred to modify the images of many of the men who participated in that debate. My purpose is not to raise a spectre from the past, but to provide an example of how powerful images of relations in an identity frame lead to the modification of episodes in ways that are difficult to justify from a 'reasonable point of view, where 'reasonableness' rests on the assumption that one of the first obligations of the state is to provide food for the malnourished, when this can be done. One might advance such arguments as the lowered costs of medical care, enhanced efficiency and better quality of life in supporting such a view.

However, let us direct our attention to the image and to the way in which an episode is altered to fit events to the image.

THE EPISODE: FEEDING BLACK SCHOOLCHILDREN BY GOVERNMENT GRANT

When the National Party came to power in 1948, it was determined to take race out of brackets — and to make an issue of it — whenever it could. Notices were placed on park benches, in post offices, in railway stations, on beaches — in a multitude of places — proclaiming that facilities were reserved for particular race groups. Before the 1948 elections, every attempt was made to embarrass the Smuts government by pointing to situations in which whites had to rub shoulders with blacks: the trains in the Cape, mixed residential areas, on buses, even at work...

Similarly, race was brought to the foreground in the issue of school feeding of black children. At the time, schoolchildren were given food to improve nutrition and enhance school performance.

It was unacceptable to the National Party that blacks (Natives) should be treated in the same way as whites (Europeans). The basis of their policy was *difference*. They had exploited the mismatch between the public image of a proper discrimination between black and white and the failure of the United Party to carry this out in all things. They simplified and purified the image — made a better gestalt of it — and satisfied the electorate's passion for simplicity, meaning, order, superiority and material advantage.

To understand the image of the party more completely we have to refer to implicit schemes, to the responses of men whose Calvinism demanded the purification of the nation (de Klerk, 1975). The interests served by this image were various: obviously, there were material interests; but in addition there were existential advantages. Apartheid and the task of building the people (*Volk*) had a religious and emancipatory significance. To lose touch with the nation was to lose touch with the vehicle which God had chosen for doing His work in the dark continent. The Afrikaner nationalist movement was the 'bearer of the future national state' and 'in the future Afrikaner national state [*Volkstaat*] the undivided power granted by God rests with the Afrikaner state authority...' The key ideas are that the state should be Afrikaner and that it should be the 'medium of Afrikanerdom to protect and promote its own fulfilment of calling [*roepingsvervulling*]' (Meyer, cited in de Klerk: 214–5). The foundation of group identity was terror, like the terror Laing (1962) describes in families where work is done to build up a fantasy of the external world as extraordinarily dangerous. This terror binds the group. As I shall demonstrate later in this chapter, nationalists construe the alternative to domination as annihilation. It is this terror that explains much of their activity. The ego, under such conditions, performs its synthesizing task by separating itself clearly and starkly from an 'unconscious evil identity, that which the ego is most afraid to resemble' and this evil identity is composed of 'images of the violated (castrated) body, the ethnic outgroup, and the exploited minority' (Erikson, 1968: 58).

One of the best ways of illustrating the projection of internal division onto the external world is to examine men debating a charitable action, where they have not the excuse of imminent danger to justify their hatred. Where positive and negative identity are sharply divided, as they were in Puritan Europe – or in Nationalist Afrikanerdom in 1948 and 1949 – the poor are as damned as the damned identity that lives in each of us. Naturally wicked men have to be driven to earn and those who do not earn are wicked.

As the history of the Poor Law in the nineteenth century was to prove, there is no touchstone, except the treatment of childhood, which reveals the true character of a social philosophy more clearly than the spirit in which it regards the misfortunes of those of its members who fell by the way.

and:

For, if the theme of the moralist was that an easy going indulgence undermined character, the theme of the economist was that it was economically disastrous and financially ruinous. The Poor Law is the mother of idleness, 'men and women growing so idle and proud that they will not work, but lie upon the parish wherein they dwell for maintenance.' It discourages thrift; 'if shame or fear of punishment makes man earn his daily bread, he will do no more; his children are the charge of the parish and his old age his recess from labour or care.' (Tawney, 1938: 265)

Many of the veins uncovered by Tawney are found in South African parliamentary discussions, produced by men who are still close to the convictions of Puritanism. They admonish their audience that philanthropy ruins those who receive it; that people ought to help themselves rather than rely upon the state; that the poor are not as poor as they are thought to be; and that white people cannot be expected to carry the improvident African. The subject is complicated by race, but the manner is that of the Puritan of the seventeenth and eighteenth centuries.

In 1949, when the government withdrew funds from the scheme to feed African children at school, P. W. Botha justified the action by arguing that school feeding undermines family pride, since it takes away parental responsibility. We must guard against 'crushing their national characteristics under a cloak of philanthropy' (Debates, 1949: 5091). He argued that many Natives attend school to be fed, not to learn, and that women neglect their families for gossip and idleness once they know that the schools will take care of them. Accusations of misanthropy are 'the sort of stories that we get every day...We have known this sort of talk for the past 300 years. The originators of the charge [were] Dr Philip, and Van der Kemp, and Reid, and other people who were bent on blackening and besmirching the original European population of the country, the Afrikaners who knew the Natives' 'interests' (Debates, 1949: 5081). One difficulty in accepting this argument is that assistance was not simultaneously withdrawn from white school feeding. Obviously, there are racial differences in ability to withstand the corrupting effects of assistance. A. J. R. van Rhyn argued that expenditure on Native education is excessive 'while our own European children are living in huts and are in huts at school. We are doing this while Europeans are living in certain parts of the country under worse conditions than Natives in the locations' (Debates, 1948: 1673).

What I hope to say — and what the example should make clear — is that the projection of an image onto society takes froms which are intelligible only if we assume that men are enacting the kind of battle between good and evil, between the accepted and the rejected, that is described by Erikson. A little attention to history — and to what men have said about it — shows that we, as a species, have pursued our 'interests' with amazing violence. The amazement is occasioned by the supposition that these interests are rational. But violence becomes intelligible when we assume that men are living in haunted houses whose rooms are filled with the evil fragments of their own rejected selves.

To return to the image and the consequences for policy: the identity frame could not be sacrificed, since discrimination between black and white was the foundation of nationalist success. Nor could treating black and white in the same way be tolerated, since this undermined the implications of the identity frame. School feeding would have different effects on whites and blacks. Policy had to eliminate identical treatment, therefore, and this was achieved by abolishing school feeding.

The context of the fantasized threat to Afrikaner (and

white) identity which was implied by the existence of blacks meant that blacks deserved the deal they got.

The relation between whites and blacks was transformed, at the level of consciousness, into one of 'spoiling', of over-protectiveness which had to be stopped. Blacks were to stand on their own legs while the ground was cut away from under their feet.

The first debate, on naming, focused on the identity frame in the image; the second debate, on school feeding, focused on the episode or treatment. The two are closely linked, but can be analytically separated in the way the components of a speech act are separated into propositions and indicators of illocutionary force (F (p)) by Searle (1969).

Images and the limits of choice

Even the most disillusioned and far-sighted political leader finds his decisions threatened by images — his own and others' — blundering about the wilderness of parliament, the media and the electorate like prehistoric monsters out on a last binge. Somehow, they have to be tamed or magicked into more intelligent beasts, but they are horny and old, and the wand at his disposal is hardly fit for use. At such times, there is a temptation to cry: 'Off with their heads!'

A careful study of the anatomy of images can be helpful, though it will not fill one with optimism. Stripped of everything, we discover that images are systems of constructs, often of such rigidity that we are amazed they can move at all. Constructs are more or less articulated to support the flesh of identity frames and episodes, and like Cuvier and the early anatomists, we have to say whether the animal can walk, swim or fly by examining these skeletal structures.

The theory I shall use in carrying out the examination is Kelly's theory of personal constructs, as promised at the beginning of this chapter. In particular, I shall make use of his concepts of commonality, core constructs, elaboration, dichotomy and organization. There will be a brief introduction to Kelly's theory, but only sufficient to grasp the bare outlines. Any further account would be superfluous, since excellent expositions exist in Kelly (1955, 1963) and Bannister and Fransella (1971).

CONSTRUCT THEORY

Kelly's fundamental postulate is that a person's processes are psychologically canalized by the ways in which he anticipates events. Anticipation is a process of construing replications. I have already discussed the ways in which incidents are construed as better or worse replications of images, and how the image can be either validated or invalidated by incidents. Much work is done to maintain images — we do not simply discard them the first time they are wrong — by adjusting the world to the image, rather than the image to the world. The more violent and hostile aspects of politics are often the result of this activity of adjustment — of persisting in showing that an image is right even when the odds are heavily against it. To construe is to place 'an interpretation' on an event (Kelly, 1963: 50). It is to see how it resembles other events and how it differs from them. These construals are not simply meditations or contemplations: they are forms of action, such as tasting, hitting, eating. To construe an event is to act on it in many ways — including, sometimes, conceptualizing the event in logical terms or symbolizing it by drawing diagrams, pictures or word pictures.

The properties of constructs are spelt out in the fundamental postulate, eleven corollaries, and comments on the formal aspects of constructs (Bannister and Fransella, 1971: 202-8, contains a useful summary).

As much as is required for the immediate purposes of this book will be given below in the discussion of each property of construct systems.

The main thing to grasp is that construct systems are

organized for the purpose of anticipating events, and directing action.

COMMONALITY

Kelly's commonality corollary can contribute substantially to our understanding of the activities of collective agents.

Commonality is defined as follows:

To the extent that one person employs a construction of experience which is similar to that employed by another, his psychological processes are similar to those of the other person. (1963: 90)

In a definite domain, commonality of construing is expected of members of the same political party. There are parties of convenience — to some extent, all parties must be parties of convenience — but to the extent that the members of a party show commonality even where it is not directly required by the immediate situation, they are likely to be difficult to break up. Parties of convenience, on the other hand, are easily destroyed by changing fortunes. The basis of understanding in the former case is so much wider than it is in the latter. In the former kind of party, members are likely to share the same kind of identity and to seek the same kinds of self-confirmations in a wide variety of actions. They are likely to have many core constructs in common. Such parties grow out of a common class or national position. They are *national* parties or *class* parties. In South Africa, the National Party has not confined itself to bread-and-butter issues: it has been concerned with the identity of the Afrikaner as opposed to other identities in South Africa. The nature of its policy — separate development or apartheid — has called for sharp distinction between itself and others, based on a construction of Afrikaner identity. Religion, language, a common history (the exemplary identity of the trekker and the symbolic history of the Great Trek are pivotal in Afrikaner identity), have been used by the National

Party in its political struggle. It is the party which has promoted the separate identity of the Afrikaner. On the other hand, there is at present no party which promotes the identity of the English speaker in South Africa. He has no history, no common religion, and his language has no particular place in his folk mythology. There is no great historical event like the Great Trek to refer to, and there are no exemplary heroes. His identity has been, till now, secured in other places, by the British Empire and the British Commonwealth. His leaders were educated in England and have commonly left South Africa for England or other English-speaking countries when South Africa became unpalatable. This is the present position. Within South Africa, there has never been any great event, such as the achievement of an English Republic, or the introduction of his own language in schools, or its acceptance as an official language, that he could look forward to as a sign that his purposes were blessed or favoured by God. He has never even been on particularly intimate terms with God, as the leaders of all great national movements seem to be.

Commonality is the basis of political power. The more far-reaching it is, the more cohesive a party is likely to be. Equally important and obvious from this discussion, is that political agents are limited in their movement by the need to achieve commonality. The political leader has to navigate a very clumsy craft and he can only do so when there is substantial agreement on the destination.

CORE CONSTRUCTS

Political agents would not survive without *core constructs*, which determine their crucial interpretations of themselves and others.

Kelly's definition is as follows:

Core constructs are those which govern a person's maintenance processes — that is, those by which he maintains his identity and existence. (1955: 482)

Peripheral constructs can be modified without significantly affecting a person's identity. Collective agents can, like persons, be defined in terms of peripheral and core constructs. Core constructs are images of the relation of members of the collective to others. The test of a core construct is that the collective begins to disintegrate if the core construct is invalidated. Morale declines after invalidation and must be restored to maintain the collective. To take an earlier example: the valour of a regiment in combat may be a core construct in maintaining it as an efficient fighting unit. Other matters of significance may be its discipline, turnout, the feeling that 'the regiment cares for its members' and 'others' care for the regiment; these will vary in the degree to which they are core or peripheral. If the regiment proves cowardly in battle, though, it begins to disintegrate as a fighting unit, unless it is able to re-establish its reputation almost immediately. The shame of the regiment will be felt by all its members – even by those who displayed courage. It has to do with the image of the collective and its relations to others. Individuals may feel that it is impossible to continue as members of the regiment. As de Gaulle observed, this is also true of the state:

...a State which cannot guarantee the defence of the nation is doomed. Neither the two French empires, nor the German empire, nor the Russian empire was able to survive defeat. Therein lies the basic legitimacy of the State. (Malraux, 1970: 100)

How does one discover the core constructs of a political agent?

Firstly, we look at what it does. The record of the National Party is fairly clear. It removed blacks from all central political processes and passed a large variety of Acts to prevent them from gaining political or economic power, as well as Acts which emphasized the complete separation of white and black wherever notions of equality might creep in.

Some of the Acts are listed below:

Group Areas Act No. 41 of 1950:
   Separate areas and territories according to race group.
Population Registration Act of 1950:
   Race classification and registration required.
Prohibition of Mixed Marriages Act of 1949:
   Forbids marriage between people of different races.
Bantu Laws Amendment Act of 1964:
   Africans' rights in areas outside homeland are restricted.
Bantu Universities Act of 1959:
   Restricts Africans to certain Universities.
Industrial Conciliation Act of 1956:
   Prohibits mixed trade unions.
Legislation on Education (various):
   Reserved education on grounds of race.
Segregation (ordinances, orders and regulations):
   Municipal and Provincial ordinances on transport and amenities; ministerial orders and regulations on medical and nursery services, employment, libraries, theatres, stores, sport, etc, etc.

The second way in which the core construct of a collective agent is shown is its composition. If a collective is supposedly open to everyone but draws only on a very limited section of the population then we can assume that the social characteristic of members are critical to its identity. Blacks cannot join the National Party. All white South Africans can, though originally the party was intended for white Afrikaners only. Nationalist members of Parliament are overwhelmingly Afrikaans-speaking.

The third way in which core constructs are discovered is by reference to *clear cases*. The logic is that discussed earlier, in looking at identity frames. Clear cases are statements which would be frequently found and not contradicted (regarded as wrong) by other members of the party, at least in their public utterances.

Here is an example of a clear case, in which Mr Vorster states a component of the core construct of the Party.

What is our policy? Surely hon. members opposite recall how many clashes we have had about it in this House. We said that in this Parliament only the representatives of the Whites would remain. We did not merely say this; we saw to it that this was what happened...(Debates, 1973: 1554)

A fourth way in which we discover the core constructs of a collective agent, such as a political party, is to study what remains constant in its policy statements and what is emphasized in the guiding principles of the party. The fundamental goals of the National Party are clear: segregation, separate identity and a Christian civilization. The achievement of the Republic was also a core construct (Mulder and Cruywagen, 1968).

Modification of various aspects of the image can be attempted, but the core remains unchanged. The limits on variation can be clearly seen in this speech of a nationalist MP, Mr Piet Marais, in which he talks about the mistakes of Nationalist policy and about adaptations which are necessary for the future. Dr Malan, he says, did brilliant work, but in that time 'we hung up apartheid signs in post offices and lifts. Now we are removing them.' J. G. Strydom was a wonderful patriot, who rejected all forms of discrimination over Afrikaners, 'yet he spoke openly to non-whites of permanent subjection' (*Baasskap en blywende heerskappy*). Dr Verwoerd brought the Republic and the homelands policy. Mr Vorster's achievements were remarkable, yet he made two basic mistakes: one was 'the removal of Coloured representation from Parliament' and the other was that he adhered to the 1936 boundaries of the reserves instead of 'trying to draw clearer borders on the map of South Africa' (*Die Burger*, 6 September 1979).

What cannot change is 'nationhood, because from the perspective of survival this is the crux'. By 'nationhood', he means white nationhood.

THE ELABORATION OF CONSTRUCTS

Images can be developed by elaborating what was implicit in its constructs.

Kelly's *choice corollary* states:

A person chooses for himself that alternative in a dichotomized construct through which he anticipates the greatest possibility for the elaboration of his system. (Kelly, 1963: 64)

In the words of Bannister and Fransella:

Kelly pointed out that the elaboration may take the form of definition (confirming in ever greater detail aspects of experience that have already been fairly actively construed), or extension (reaching out to increase the range of the construct system by exploring new areas that are only very partially understood). It must be stressed, however, that elaboration is sought in terms of the system as it exists at the time and that the choice corollary does not imply that we always successfully elaborate. We can over-define to the point where we suffer the death of ultimate boredom, circling in a ritual manner around the same area, or we can overreach the system and suffer death by ultimate chaos. (1971: 25–26)

Strictly speaking, the choice corollary makes allowance only for choosing one or other pole of an existing construct. It does not tell us how a 'new' construct comes into existence. Theorists like Piaget (and Kelly) have always insisted that the ensemble, the system of operations or constructs, has to be understood if we are to explain action and change. It may be that when we look at an ensemble of constructs we can see that the novel choice is not very surprising. The question often becomes: what *prevented* the person (or a group of persons) from using that construct before?

I want to consider the development of the concept of multi-nationalism in National Party policy. A good starting point is 20 January 1948, when Dr Malan, who will become prime minister after the elections, is speaking on the Representation of Natives and Indians in the House of Assembly. He is arguing against any representation. He is also arguing against the Native Representatives' Council, because the native groups in this country do not form a nation but will, if the Native Representatives' Council continues to exist, be formed into one. He proposes instead that different groups should be given their own, separate institutions, which will concern themselves with their own tribal affairs. He raises the old South African plea that they should 'lift the Native problem out of party politics', by which he means that the Natives should have no place in the national political system. He refers to the danger of communist agitators who wish to persuade blacks that they form one nation.

When we examine the elements of this speech, it is quite clear that there are many that have been absolutely constant in National Party thinking. The first constant is that there shall be no representation of 'non-whites' in the House of Assembly. Then there is the idea that South Africa is not inhabited by a single nation — and even more important, the Natives are not to be allowed to form a single nation. The concept of separate political authorities was advanced. Segregation as advocated in this speech, has been the foundation of National Party policy.

Now, what has changed? Very little, or a great deal, depending on one's point of view. Most people would, I think, say very little. The concept of separate political authorities has been taken a step further. In other words, the construct: single nation/separate nations has been constant and the pole chosen has been constant. The meaning of 'separate nations' was expanded to imply *separate states* by Dr Verwoerd, which is something Malan did not envisage, at least in this speech. One might say that this was an inevitable consequence — provided the choice was not reversed, and the members of the party did not decide that they would rather have a single nation than face the consequence of separate states. But this move was blocked by the impossibility of accepting a single nation which would include blacks and whites, and hence the impossibility of a single citizenship.

The impossibility of single citizenship is strongly stated by Dr Malan in a speech to the House on 22 September 1948. He has now become prime minister, and he takes up the themes of his January pre-election speech. Social equality and the abolition of colour bars are race suicide.

The Prime Minister:

Her [Mrs Ballinger's] view is that all colour bars in the country must disappear. Her view is that there should be absolutely no discrimination in any field in South Africa between one race group and another race group. Her standpoint is that of absolute equality. The democracy that she stands for is this: give to everyone in South Africa, without distinction of race or colour, the same political rights and the same franchise for the same legislative body. Give them representation here in the Assembly and in the Senate.

Mr Klopper:* Shame.

The Prime Minister:* Well, she remains consistent. That is her standpoint. We know her standpoint, but I ask her whether white South Africa will ever accept it.

Hon. Members:* No.

The Prime Minister:* Should the day break when South Africa is prepared to accept it, then South Africa will be destroying itself, and I believe that the day never will dawn in South Africa so long as white South Africa still wishes to make its future safe in South Africa; the day will never dawn when they will be ready to commit race-suicide.

We can look at outside events which helped to form the decision to follow out the implication that separate nations require separate states. There was the fact that neighbouring states were gaining independence, and that racial oppression was no longer acceptable to the world. There was the reassuring observation that an independent Botswana,

* Translated.

Swaziland and Lesotho were not in a position to do much damage. Furthermore, one might extract cheap labour from independent states and feel morally on a par with European states which were doing the same. The governments of the separate states would be responsible for their own problems of law and order.

The choice which was made, in terms of multi-nationalism, can then be seen as quite consistent with a system of ideas which had already been in existence for a long time. An added advantage of this elaboration was that equality between members of different nations did not immediately threaten the control which the white man exercised in his own area.

Finally, though, members of the National Party retain a pool of several unchanged constructs. These are the constructs they apply to the relations between white and black *after* the separation of states. The constructs enunciated by Malan before the 1948 election remain the constructs which are being defined and redefined in the present. There is racial inequality, no representation in the House of Assembly, and the threat of agitators.

But, when we attempt to understand the choices men make, it is not enough to refer to the choice corollary.

To gain a better understanding of the way in which alternatives are construed and then limit movement, I have undertaken a detailed investigation of the Debates of the House of Assembly of the Republic of South Africa (or, Union of South Africa as it was in the earlier material of the study). The subject of the Debates was local African affairs and the years studied were 1948, 1958 and 1968. Sampling over a period of twenty years gave an opportunity to see how constructs had changed. The year 1948 was chosen because that was the year the National Party — the party that has been in power ever since — came into power.

The goal of this study should be made clear. It is to give an example of the construing of an image and it is not an attempt to give a detailed history of South African politics, which has been written about frequently by various sociologists and historians. This is an attempt to show how political psychology might be done.

DICHOTOMY

We see that the choice corollary refers to 'dichotomized' constructs. The elaboration of one alternative in such a construct is a way of developing an image. To understand why development is limited to one alternative we have to understand what lies at the other pole of the construct.

Kelly believed that:

A person's construction system is composed of a finite number of dichotomous constructs. (1963: 59)

There is a reason to doubt the universal validity of this statement: Strawson's distinction between categorizing and characterizing statements makes one limitation clear, and the semantics of multinary systems of classification, such as systems of colours or metals, is difficult to reconcile with this view. Nevertheless, in party politics, decision often takes place in a matrix of alternatives. Choices are polarized. The dynamics of this polarization can be understood by reference to Erikson's comments on the separation of the self from the unconscious evil identity, cited earlier, particularly where the group is threatened. The threat may be objective or fantasized or both.

In political life, it is seldom possible to examine all possible choices.

We must usually rest content with the pool of alternatives as they are construed in a particular political system.

In day-to-day debate, we see issues posed as either/or decisions. There is, in the background, also a pool of quite different constructions of reality which are excluded, either because the representatives of these views could not gain enough votes to enter the House of Assembly, or because the representatives of these views have been silenced in some more violent way, by being banned or exiled. This follows from the fact that radical change requires, not merely the reversal of a construct, but the advocacy of a completely different construction of events. (Kelly's (1962) paper on *Europe's Matrix of Decision* is particularly valuable.)

When we know the system of alternatives, as they are construed by practising politicians, we may frequently understand why a particular construction of an event is maintained after repeated invalidation. We may also understand political practice better if we realize that validation requires a subjective compatibility between an outcome and a prediction, which means that we have to understand the *use* which the person is making of a particular construct. The use may not be what we believe it is. This is a common feature of human activity. In politics, men may construe events in a particular way to gain power, and this may validate their construction of events though this construction seems to be leading to disaster. In fact, the event they are construing is not the event we think they are construing. Yet, whatever the private beliefs of practitioners, this system of public constructs gains momentum and has consequences. It acts as the grid within which political action occurs. To this extent, the private convictions of the practitioners are irrelevant. It is their public construction that is politically significant.

There is always a complicated relation between private conviction and political convenience, a relation that has formed the basis of political commentary since Machiavelli. Where politicians are close to the people they represent, they may be able to win favour more spontaneously. But the construction of events, once it has become the investment of a party, has its own reality and imposes its own constraints.

In the present study the dichotomy corollary was applied

to establish a set of clear and representative statements of the alternatives on various issues. Some of these were statements of policy. Should we establish industries in the border areas or in the existing urban areas? Should South Africa be treated as a single state or should it be broken up into several states? And then, closely tied up with statements of policy are statements of consequence, which are essentially reasons for doing or not doing things. What are the consequences of establishing industries in existing urban areas? What are the consequences of preserving the integrity of the Republic?

These are the sorts of terms that Gerth and Mills call *motives* in their discussion of the vocabulary of motivation, following Max Weber. They state that 'strategic choice of motive is part of the attempt to motivate the act for the *other* persons involved in our conduct. Carefully chosen and publicised motives often resolve social conflicts, potential and real, and thus effectively integrate and release social patterns of "conduct"' (1954: 117). Motives are 'terms which persons typically use in their interpersonal relations', especially when there are 'alternative or unexpected purposes or conduct' (p. 114).

What Gerth and Mills call *motives* are here called *constructs*. The observations apply exactly. Constructions of events are publicized to 'integrate and release social patterns of conduct', especially where there are 'alternative or unexpected purposes or conduct'. The arrangement of Parliament ensures that there are alternative and unexpected courses of action. Even more strongly, there are contested purposes and actions. The spelling out of alternatives is part of the structure of the motive.

Representative constructions of alternatives were extracted in the following way. First, the policy of the party was studied carefully. Then, the debates were read and alternatives as they were *typically* posed by members were extracted. Idiosyncratic statements were ignored because, though they might be interesting to the individual, they did not reveal the *commonality* that is necessary in political action. A party is a machine for achieving commonality in its public construction of events, and a severe discipline is imposed on members in all important issues.

We can compare this to the linguist's use of *clear cases* when he is exhibiting the structure of a linguistic argument. He finds examples which are widely shared; even more important, people who are native speakers of the language (and even more specifically, of the dialect) accept the statement as a clear case. In the current study, the 'speakers of the dialect' were members of the National Party, the United Party, the Progressive Party (only one, in 1968), and, for a while, the Native Representatives. A *clear case* was a case that was not contradicted by others in the party, or by the individual himself. The result is a pool of statements of quite unexceptional dullness.

At first, the dictionary of alternatives contained a large number of items (300), but it turned out that very few of these were used with great consistency (120). The dictionary may seem small to cover so many years of political debate, but the essence of political debate is simplicity. The total number of tokens (classifications using the dictionary) was 3,551, and the total number of arguments was 1,065. These apparently superfluous figures were useful in examining the depth of argument in different parties.

The most frequently used dictionary items are given below:

African events (contrast: local, other foreign)
African identity (contrast: lose identity, imitation whites, civilized people)
African interests (contrast: harm African interests; white interests)
African tax (contrast: pay less tax; irresponsibility)
African welfare (contrast: slums; crime; poverty; disintegration of family life)

assist Africans (contrast: assist whites; avoid charity)
backward blacks (contrast: civilized whites; skilled blacks)
black domination (contrast: white domination: separate autonomy)
black urban rights (contrast: black rural rights; no black urban rights)
border industries (contrast: homeland industries; urban industries)
bureaucratic control (contrast: parliamentary control; reduce red tape)
common advantage (contrast: sectional, group advantage)
common university education (contrast: tribal colleges)
common parliament (contrast: no representation; separate parliaments; satellites)
communism (contrast: nationalism; capitalism; freedom; South African way of life)
conflict (contrast: white control; accept segregation, intimidated)
constitution (contrast: will of people; betrayal)
consult (contrast: govern; ignore wishes)
cost or efficiency (contrast: ideology; ignore facts; pursue greater interest)
democratic values (contrast: binding constitution; fail to consult; ignore spirit of constitution)
economic integration (contrast: job reservation; border industries, stagnation, industrialize homelands)
full employment (contrast: unrest; poverty; economic stagnation)
growth (contrast: stagnation; unrest)
homelands, separate (contrast: integration; national suicide; traditional South African segregation)
laissez faire (white enterprise) (contrast: stagnation; bureaucratic bungling; planned development of homelands and border industries)
migrant workers (contrast: black domination; integration; skilled, stable population)

136 IMAGES

miscegenation (contrast: immorality act; racial purity; traditional segregation)

misinform outside world (contrast: patriotism; government behaves more responsibly)

morality (contrast: inhumanity; indifference)

nationalism, recognize (contrast: lack realism; chaos; political immorality; realism)

parliamentary sovereignty, will of people (contrast: binding constitution; right of minorities; delegate control; government by bureaucracy and executive)

paternalism (contrast: natives exploited; freedom)

petty apartheid (contrast; grand apartheid; traditional way of life; freedom; economic development; morality, integration)

population balance (contrast: black majority; black movement to cities; failure to gain white immigrants)

poverty, African (contrast: less petty apartheid; more economic development; less regulation of economy, deny poverty)

property segregation (contrast; immorality; crime; integration)

race identification (contrast: political and social integration)

rule of law, social apartheid (contrast: mixed amenities, residence, integration)

survival (contrast: loss of political control; loss of culture and nationhood; physical extermination)

urban labour (contrast: economic stagnation; develop homelands)

wage control, minimum (contrast: job reservation; poverty)

Westernize (contrast: African identity; poverty; barbarism)

white control (contrast: black domination)

white workers, welfare (contrast: abandon job reservation; economic development of reserves and border industries)

world opinion (contrast: reject world opinion; preserve own way of life; isolation)

This short dictionary accounts for about ninety per cent of the entries. A particularly important feature of the dictionary is its bipolarity, so that each entry may, by linking it with a specific contrast, show the alternatives as they were construed by the speaker. In some cases the alternative was not clear; in Kelly's terminology the pole is submerged, and it would take a personal interview to discover how the speaker construed the alternative. From a dictionary of this sort one gets a clear idea not only of what constructs were used with what frequency, but also what dimensions of analysis were employed. Parties may be distinguished from each other and movements within parties may be traced across time.

Some idea of the extent of the sample may be gained from the number of speeches read and analysed.

1948 (1st session, 10th Parliament): 165 speeches.

1958 (1st session, 12th parliament): 217 speeches.

1968 (3rd session, 3rd Parliament): 303 speeches.

The number of speeches devoted to Native (Bantu) affairs showed a steady increase commensurate with the number of Acts. There was a usual core of reference during the No Confidence Debate, Prime Minister's Vote, Departmental Votes, and Part Appropriation.

The parties studied are given below:
1948 and 1958: National Party
United Party
Native Representatives
1968: National Party
United Party
Progressive Party

The Native Representatives were abolished before 1968. Smaller parties, such as the Afrikaner Party and the Labour Party, were absorbed into the two main parties and have not been studied as separated entities.

Some comments on this dictionary are worth making. The most obvious feature of the dictionary is that it looks untidy and in some cases trivial. This is true. It is the nature of day-to-day debate. It is also a consequence of dismemberment in this way. When things are broken up the parts often look silly, or at least useless. When they are put together as images — whole constructions which represent the present, the future, or the past — they become significant. Often the whole is not mentioned in a particular speech — it lingers in the background. The issue — the particular alternative in question — has to be interpreted against this whole.

But I hope that the use I shall make of the dictionary — of the parts — will justify the labour that went into constructing it. The dictionary on its own would not be sufficient to give a picture, but the picture can be seen more vividly after analysis.

In Table 3 I give the constructs which are used most frequently by the various parties.

From this analysis we can see how the parties construe reality.

To explore still further the differences between the parties and changes within the parties, they may be compared on the main dimensions of the table taken separately. The main dimensions of comparison are (a) white identity and survival; (b) African identity and survival; (c) the threat of conflict; (d) economic interest; (e) African welfare and (f) moral and ethical arguments. The integrity of the constitution will not be pursued: it was peculiar to the period in which many constitutional changes were introduced.

The comparison may be given a quantitative form by taking from the dictionary those types which bear on the dimension of comparisons and entering the frequency with which they were used by members of each party. Starting with white identity and survival, several items in the dictionary clearly relate.

White identity and survival: survival
　　　　　　　　　　　　　black domination
　　　　　　　　　　　　　communism
　　　　　　　　　　　　　white control

Table 3: *Constructs used most frequently by each party (contrast in brackets)*

	National	United	Native Representatives[1]/ Progressive[2]
1948	survival (lose control, exterminated)	constitution (betray)	African welfare (slums; broken families poverty)
	African identity (lose identity; imitation white man)		morality (inhumanity)
1958	survival (lose control; (lose culture; exterminated)	cost and efficiency (ideology; ignore facts)	African welfare (slums; broken families poverty)
			morality (inhumanity)
1968	survival (lose control; lose culture)	cost and efficiency (ideology; ignore facts)	African welfare (slums; broken families poverty)
	conflict (white control; accept segregation)		morality (inhumanity)
	African identity (lose identity; imitation white man)		

[1] Native Representatives were abolished before 1968.
[2] The Progressive Party was not in existence in 1948 and 1958.

To make comparison across parties and years possible, scores are converted to percentages according to the following formula:

$$\frac{\text{Total number of 'white survival' arguments in given party in given year}}{\text{Total number of arguments in given party in given year}} \times 100$$

Differences in the sizes of the parties and the number of speakers are ruled out.

Table 4 shows how the parties compared across the years in their use of the argument that white survival entails certain policies.

Table 4: *Per cent appeal to white survival in arguing policy*

	National	United	Native Representatives	Progressive
1948	35	6	0	—
1958	30	12	0	—
1968	15	14	—	8

As expected, the National Party used the argument rather more than other parties did, but the threat of communism and of black domination was used to an increasing extent by the United Party. The result is that by 1968 the two parties are almost level. There remains a difference. In the Nationalist argument the contrast of survival is frequently cultural extinction of the Afrikaner; in United Party argument the contrast is frequently loss of control and more rarely extinction of Western civilization.

What is unexpected and interesting about the figures is the decline in the use of white survival as an argument in the National Party. The decline is substantial.

The next theme (Table 5) is African identity. Only two dictionary entries were used for calculating the importance of this argument: African identity and nationalism. As before, scores were converted to percentages.

The tildes in front of the 2 and the 5 on the bottom row indicate that the United Party and the Progressive Party

Table 5: *Per cent appeal to African identity in arguing policy*

	National	United	Native Representatives	Progressive
1948	11	0	0	–
1958	1	0	0	–
1968	11	~2	–	~5

rejected policies which might lead to separate African identity. They saw such separate identity as a threat rather than as a desirable goal. If we disregard the drop in 1958, the achievement of distinctive African identity and the recognition of black nationalism are desirable goals to the Nationalists.

African identity is used to argue *against* a 'white' education for Africans, detribalization and a free drift to town, charity which will make Africans dependent on government handouts; and *for* social segregation, development of the reserves, and the development of tribal and traditional characteristics. This was in 1948. In 1968, the argument still had many of these functions. It is used to argue against educational integration at universities, and *for* social apartheid, homeland (reserve) development, border industries, and shifting most school development to the homelands. Recognizing black nationalism has come to have a more positive function than African identity *per se*: it introduces the new principles of autonomy and of separate government. The *preservation* of African identity is a more defensive, conservative principle than the recognition of nationalism. The former often involved attempts to fix African character and custom; the latter contains the seeds of the future. The former is nostalgic and often paternalist; the latter contains a new respect. The former is contained in the following statement: 'Once the detribalized and westernized Native returns for a while to his own people, he soon realizes what he really is' (M. S. F. Grobler, 1958). The latter is contained in the statement that 'self-realization is the inalienable right of each and every nation' (M. C. Botha, 1968).

The third theme (Table 6) is the threat of conflict, which makes certain policies necessary. Averting racial tension, disturbances of the peace, riots, and internal dissension are often presented as arguments for policies.

Table 6: *Per cent appeal to threat of conflict in arguing policy*

	National	United	Native Representatives	Progressive
1948	2	1	0	—
1958	5	4	0	—
1968	9	5	—	5

In all parties there has been a rise in the urgency of finding solutions which will avoid conflict. The National Party, which stresses survival, also stresses the need to avoid conflict more than any other party does.

The fourth theme (Table 7) involves assessment of the material costs of a policy and the policy's efficiency in reducing these costs. This is most generally expressed as an interest in the economics of political action. Under this heading the following dictionary entries are included.

Economic interests: cost and efficiency
     growth
     urban labour
     laissez faire
     full employment
     white workers

Economic interests are to be interpreted in a fairly broad sense, though predominantly from the white point of view. *Cost and efficiency* does refer to social costs which might not normally be included in a strict economic analysis.

In spite of the increase in economic participation of the Afrikaner, economic interests do not take a larger share of

Table 7: *Per cent appeal to economic interests in arguing policy*

	National	United	Native Representatives	Progressive
1948	9	15	20	—
1958	11	52	20	—
1968	8	22	—	16

the National Party argument in 1968 than in 1948. The National Party still places other things first in motivating policy towards Africans. Both opposition parties emphasize economic interests to a very much greater extent.

African welfare (Table 8) is a theme of some importance in the arguments of the Native Representatives and Progressive Party. It is of interest to see how prominently it has featured in the arguments of other parties. The dictionary items included are shown below.

African welfare: African interests
African welfare
assist Africans
poverty, African

Table 8: *Per cent appeal to African welfare in arguing policy*

	National	United	Native Representatives	Progressive
1948	0	8	34	—
1958	3	13	43	—
1968	5	10	—	20

There is an obvious 'welfare gradient' across the parties. The major government reaction to African poverty has been to deny it, whereas the other parties have made this the basis of many strong appeals for succour. There has been a slight increase in the tendency of government speakers to motivate policy by reference to African welfare, though, and this is consonant with changes in the implementation of separate development. Observers still (in 1979) tend to observe more separation than development in government action, though there is now talk of consolidating the homelands in order to make them viable states.

It is difficult, in the absence of consolidated figures, to show the degree of success or failure of the government in developing black areas. As an illustration of failure, one might take unemployment, acting on the assumption that one of the major functions of an economic system is to provide employment for those seeking work. All the figures given below are drawn from *A Survey of Race Relations in South Africa 1977*, published by the South African Institute of Race Relations. They are based on the calculations of Professor P. J. van der Merwe. When we compare black unemployment in urban and rural areas (whether the rural areas are in 'white' or 'black' territory), we find that, in urban areas, unemployment was sensitive to the economic boom of the early 70s, falling during that period, whereas in rural areas unemployment has risen steadily since 1970. In white rural areas the figures for 1970 and 1976 are 25,000 and 401,000 unemployed; in black rural areas the comparable figures are 32,000 and 437,000 unemployed. In urban areas, the figures for 1970 and 1976 are 227,000 and 222,000 unemployed, with a decline in unemployment during the early 70s (p. 214).

What can be said of all these figures is that black unemployment is considerable and that the homelands are no better or worse off than white rural areas. There is no prospect, at the moment, of full employment, due to the relatively slow rate of economic growth (a world problem) and a rate of increase in the black population which is twice the rate of increase in the white population.

All these figures have to be evaluated against a background of global unemployment and economic stagnation.

Finally, ethical argument crops up more frequently in the

arguments of some parties than in the arguments of others. Some indication of frequency is given in Table 9 below.

Table 9: *Per cent appeal to morality in arguing policy*

	National	United	Native Representatives	Progressive
1948	0	5	18	—
1958	0	0	6	—
1968	1	4	—	10

In drawing up this table, only specific appeals to humanity, decency or morality were taken into account. The category was kept narrow to prevent its becoming a ragbag into which all welfare arguments could be dropped.

THE ORGANIZATION COROLLARY

Having dealt with the parts, we shall now try to deal with their organization, because it is as whole systems that they are generally useful to individuals.

Kelly's *Organization Corollary* states:

Each person characteristically evolves for his convenience in anticipating events, a construction system embracing ordinal relationships between constructs. (1963: 56)

The first application which I shall make of this corollary will be to examine the ordinal relation between constructs. The second will be to see what kind of picture is made up of the parts.

Let us consider firstly the ordinal relation of constructs.

Where there is an ordinal relation between constructs, one construct may be justified in terms of another. The closer the relation, the more use will be made of justifications, drawing upon those constructs which are more fundamental. Thus, the production of connected argument reflects relations within the construct system — its connectedness. But argument is not always necessary, even though the form of the debate would seem to encourage it. Reiteration may be sufficient. Emphasis may be used. However, as a situation becomes more complicated — which means that our construction of it has to be modified — there is more and more room for unexpected courses of action. The unexpected has to be justified. Or, let us say — since there is nothing to compel a politician to justify what he is doing — the unexpected needs explaining. This also follows from what Gerth and Mills said about motives; that they are 'terms which persons typically use in their interpersonal relations', especially when there are 'alternative or unexpected purposes or conduct' (Gerth and Mills, 1954: 114). It follows that, in complicated situations — and a complicated situation is one which requires a modification of image — more connected argument should be produced by persons trying to decide what to do or to justify what they have decided to do. This is, of course, an empirical statement which needs evidence.

I am proposing that connectedness is, among other things, an index of the awareness of the person that he is confronting a changing situation and that he has to do something which is not obvious. The quality of connectedness is not what I am judging here. I am interested — for the purpose of this index — in quantity.

Where events are not problematic, where there is a transparently correct construction of events, no reasons need be given for any particular decision. This can occur when events are construed in a constellatory or a pre-emptive manner. Under constellatory construing, if something is identified in one way, then all its other properties are known. This is useful. It also makes expansion relatively unnecessary. Under pre-emptive construing, if a thing is known to be that thing, then it is not necessary to know anything else about it. Even more strongly, knowing something about it means that there *is* nothing else to know about it. On the other hand, propositional construing requires argument, since we have to subject our construing to test.

When referring to 'unexpected purposes or conduct' we are also saying something about commonality and sociality. Where there is a high degree of commonality between representatives and the people they are representing, they may not need to explain very much, if we assume that much of their argument is directed at the electorate. The consequences of the sociality corollary are much more difficult to predict, since it involves construing the processes of the other person; it would mean an adjustment of the argument to his grasp, finding ways of outwitting him, and so on. It is much more likely to affect the manner in which the debate is addressed to the opposition and the party in Parliament. In any case, the effects are not easy to sum up.

Now, when we examine the debates on 'Native Affairs' in 1948, we are struck by the fact that members of the National Party are stating obvious *facts*; that is, they are construing events in a way which is, for them and for the community they represent, transparently right. They are stating the *fact* that the Native must be kept in his place and that the races must be segregated. In 1968 these facts have been transformed into less obvious and more subtle forms: the policy of apartheid has become the policy of separate development, and simple racial segregation, though much the same thing, has become part of a policy of multinationalism. A reading of the debate makes it clear that the construct system has become much more complex. There are many aternative and unexpected courses of action which have to be explained and justified to anxious supporters, even if the justification is merely to take the form that things have not changed. To show that they have not changed is now a little more difficult because at the same time others have to be convinced that they have.

Concealment might be a good thing, but action is necessary and questions have to be answered. There is no way out of the elected politician's dilemma. He must construe. And as the relations between his purposes and the construct system he is using become more tenuous, the more construing he is forced to do.

What I have done here is to examine the amount of connected argument at three points in time: 1948, 1958 and 1968. I have taken this to reflect an awareness of the problematic nature of the situation. The less connected argument, the less problematic the situation, the more connected argument, the more problematic the situation. Simply reading the debates does give one the impression that in 1948 things were rather obvious to the National Party, but that events tended – especially after 1968, by which time there was much independence in Africa and the former colonial powers were scrubbing themselves as clean as possible of all former taint of racism – to blot and blur this obviousness.

How should we calculate depth of argument? Let us assume that we have our dictionary – as we have – of *types* of construct. Every time we recognize one of these constructs in a speech, we score one *token*. Sometimes these tokens are connected by logical terms, such as 'is the same as', 'has the consequence that' or 'implies' or 'negates' or 'contradicts'. These logical terms are connections between tokens.

Argument depth was calculated in this study by dividing the number of tokens into the number of connections in any one speech. This is illustrated below, using a simple argument:

Recognizing nationalism   (implies)   creating separate homelands.
Erosion in homelands   (?)   (?)

This argument occurs in one speech. The first part of the argument is clear, but the second part faded. Three tokens are scored, but only one connection: the implication in the first line.

The argument depth is calculated by the following formula:

$$\frac{\text{number of connections}}{\text{number of tokens}} \times 100$$

In this example, we get:

$$\frac{1}{3} \times 100 = .33$$

The higher the number, the greater the amount of connected argument. Simple utterance of different constructs without connecting them is complexity of a sort, but it is not argument.

The changes in the depth of argument over the time sampled are given in Table 10.

Table 10: *Mean depth of argument*

	National	United	Native	Representatives	Progressive
1948	17	36	44		—
1958	22	34	36		—
1968	32	37	—		41
Mean	24	36	40		41

There are two things to notice about this set of figures. Government (National Party) speakers produce more connected argument in recent than in earlier years; and the opposition parties all produce more connected argument than the governing National Party.

A test for uniform distribution in the scores of the National Party yields a χ^2 of 5.02 ($p < .05$). It would seem, therefore, that the trend towards connected argument is significant.

The behaviour of the opposition parties in producing more argument is also consistent with our discussion of problematic situations. The opposition is clearly not in possession of obvious truths or it would not be in opposition. The truths may, to put it differently, be obvious to the opposition, but they are not to the majority of the electorate. To that extent the situation is problematic. People have to be convinced. One way to do it is to explain. Perhaps it is the least effective way, but it is the only recourse of parties without powerful truisms at their disposal.

6
Beyond Ideology

In this chapter I want to ask the question: what is the relation between personality and personal beliefs on the one hand and social structure and ideology on the other?

There are, broadly speaking, two answers to this question. The first is the 'reflection' theory, that men are constituted by their society and its dominant ideology; the second is the 'conversation' theory, that men are intelligible in the context of their society and its dominant ideology (or, for that matter, ideologies), but that they have some part to play in constituting themselves by the use they make of the practices in which they must, willy-nilly, participate. Most people would subscribe to some version of the second view. The first is found mainly in implicit forms, as an assumption or a mode of political confusion, as when a man's arguments are discredited by saying that they simply reflect his class position. The advantages of this move, from the point of view of those who represent 'the people' or 'the workers', is that their views are thought to have the broadest base and, therefore, to be more valid. Often, the base is asserted by definition rather than electoral test. This view I shall call *sociologism*, and it is worth stating it in full, in order to exorcize it.

But before doing so, I must say more about the second, 'conversation' theory. This answer might be said to be 'dialectical', if we could attach any useful meaning to the word. A better answer might be that individuals become agents by using the tools they discover in society, and that once they are agents they are able to discover new uses for old tools and even, occasionally, new tools. The process is rather like that of learning to use language. We learn to use the language of our community, but we do end up saying the things we want to say. Perhaps, in most cases, these are not very original things; but, nevertheless, they are occasionally our own things. What we say is intelligible in context (including the context of the words of other participants in a conversation), but it can hardly be said to be determined by the context; nor can it be said to simply 'reflect' the context. Conversation takes account of the context, is relevant to the context, is appropriate to the context, and many other similar things, but it does not simply 'reflect' the context and it cannot be said to be 'determined' by the context, for reasons which I shall discuss in greater detail later. Similarly, to understand persons and ideology we have to understand the social context in which they arise; but the relation between a person and her social context is 'conversational'. She is intelligible in a social context, related to it in some way – but she is not a reflection of it nor is she determined by it. This is the second kind of answer to the question of how persons and their beliefs are constituted.

I shall now state the first answer in detail.

Sociologism

A strong form of sociologism is found in Marx's sixth thesis on Feuerbach, which states:

The human essence is no abstraction inherent in each individual. In its reality it is the ensemble of social relations. (Marx, 1975: 423)

We can take this as a convenient starting point in order to pin down a troublesome assumption. A little later, in presenting Sève's views, I shall give Marxist theory a hearing.

Sociologism can be clearly understood by stating it as Fodor states *behaviourism*:

To qualify as a behaviorist in the broad sense of the term I shall employ, one need only believe that the following proposition expresses a necessary truth: For each mental predicate that can be employed in a psychological explanation, there must be at least one description of behavior to which it bears a logical connection. (Fodor, 1968: 51)

A careful reading of this shows that there are several different psychological explanations that qualify as behaviourist under this definition, which is referred to as P in the following passage:

What makes a doctrine behaviorist is that it follows that if the doctrine is true then P is true necessarily. The necessity of P is entailed by (but does not entail) all those doctrines that have been called behaviorist; doctrines such as: 'Mental events require behavioral criteria' (Wittgenstein); 'Intervening variables must be tied to observables "at both ends"' (Hull; 'theoretical terms in psychology must be eliminable in favour of terms that designate observables' (general reductionism); 'mental statements are dispositional statements' (Ryle); 'explanations of behavior must not refer to events taking place at "other levels of observation"' (Skinner)...In its most radical and simple form behaviorism asserts that all mental concepts are directly reducible to behavioral concepts, i.e., explicit definition can be given for each mental concept on terms of observables. A softer form of behaviorism argues that the necessary and sufficient conditions for the application of mental terms must be specifiable in behavioral terms. This is to say that behaviorists differ about the nature of the supposed logical connection between mental and behavioral predicates. (N. Mackay, 1975: 225–6)

The mentalist is then a man who denies 'necessarily P', where P is the definition given by Fodor. When we discuss behaviourism as a set of practices, as Koch does, we see that

these practices embody the logic of P. The practices and 'orientative attitudes' of behaviourism are the following (Koch, 1954):
1 The insistence on intersubjective techniques for securing and expressing empirical data.
2 The advocacy of stimulus and response variables as the only legitimate independent and dependent variables in which to express the results of psychological research and formulate theory.
3 The commitment to conditioned response principles or some related form of S–R associationism as the basic law of learning.
4 A strong emphasis on 'peripheral' determinants of behavior.
5 An emphasis on extreme environmentalism.

It will be seen that the pivot of the behaviourist approach is its emphasis on stimulus and response variables and environment control of behaviour.

This statement of the nature of behaviourism (in which I have leant heavily on N. Mackay, 1975) is introduced simply to enable me to state an analogous doctrine, sociologism. Sociologism can be stated as follows, by analogy with Fodor's definition of behaviourism as a philosophical and scientific doctrine:

Sociologism is the doctrine that: for each mental or behavioural predicate that can be employed in a psychological explanation, there must be at least one description of society to which it bears a logical connection.

In its most radical and simple form, sociologism asserts that all psychological concepts are directly reducible to statements about society and social organization. Of course, theorists will differ in their analysis of the crucial social determinants of behaviour and of mental states, but they will agree that this is the only way to do social psychology. We may call this definition S.

We saw that a mentalist was someone who denied

'necessarily P'. A psychologist is someone who denies 'necessarily S'.

How does one deny P or S?

The first way is to ask those who affirm P or S whether they affirm it as a dogma – as the only way to do social science – or as an approach in their formulation of exact hypotheses. When it takes the form of precise assertions to the effect that particular mental and psychological predicates have a logical connection to particular descriptions of society, then we can examine the nature of the logical connection. Thus we may say that ideology 'reflects' the real relations of production. But what is the nature of 'reflection'? And how do individuals come to produce and accept ideologies? What are the processes by which ideologies are seen by participants to explain the real relations of society?

In other words, the first way in which P or S can be denied is to ask those in favour to produce a science which is based on it. This is always unsatisfactory, because a view may be correct and yet not have very much to show.

I do not wish to reject P or S on the grounds of their insufficiencies or their inability to explain this or that difficult problem in psychology. Both of them seem to attribute the organization of mind and behaviour to the organization of the environment, which seems to me a risky proposition, but I know of no logical way of refuting it. Both of them are reflexive, to a limited extent, in that we can argue that revolutionary views arise in certain environments (where there are contradictions which produce contradictory ideas and emotions), but obviously this is not very persuasive. Marxist theory has great difficulty in showing that Marxist theory is not simply an ideological reflection of the environment, but on the other hand, there aren't many theories that deal particularly well with these problems.

When we ask why certain explanations are not satisfactory, when we ask how people understand the contradictions that arise, we are introducing terms that refer to the organizational powers of the individual. The individual is able to act on the environment in certain ways, and the organization of these actions is not something that can be attributed solely to the environment. There are, after all, species differences. We cannot regard the relations in the actions of the individual as being out there, in the environment, since these relations are not equally available to all individuals of the same species and — even more strongly — of different species. In other words, relations have to be studied at different levels of organization in the individual and in society. We have to have some theory about the processing of the environment by the individual. To a certain extent, the theory of operant conditioning is such a theory, but it presents an extremely poor version of the organization of behaviour. When we ask the question: could we conceivably construct a model within the theory of operant conditioning which would achieve the complex behaviour we observe in humans? — the answer must be no.

The obvious answer to both behaviourism and sociologism is that we must be allowed to theorize about the capacities of the system that can process the environment in such elaborate ways. This is particularly necessary when we consider the complex activities of logical thought, imaginative transformations of the environment in art and science, and vast species differences in the ability to transform the environment into various organized representations, as pictures, as languages, as maps, as flow-charts, and so on.

The activity of transforming the environment ideologically or scientifically or in any other way may be studied in various ways. A particularly fruitful way may be to examine the social transactions or the contingencies of reinforcement within which these discoveries are made, but such a study will be fruitful only to the extent that it rests on a theory of the ways in which the individual can discover the lessons of the environment. This is quite different from either behaviourism or sociologism. It is the study of the *use* which organisms with definite capacities can make of their environment, not only the study of the use which their environments make of them. The opposition is possible only to the extent that individuals have the power of transforming the environment in which they live: by symbolic or sensori-motor actions of various degrees of complexity.

Of course, this does not amount to a science. There are a number of essays at such a science, to be found in the special problem areas of language, the development of perception, and theories of memory, pattern recognition, and so on. Wherever there has been detailed study of a problem it has been found necessary to reject both behaviourism and sociologism. Once more, it is essential to be clear that the rejection refers to behaviourism and sociologism as logical doctrines. The study of the use of environments remains scientifically fruitful.

A Marxist view

Lucien Sève, in presenting a Marxist view of personality, arrives at a position which is intermediate between reflection theory and conversational theory. The difficulty is that he starts off with such strong sociological theses that he leaves himself little room for psychology.

His first thesis is simply Marx's 6th thesis on Feuerbach, cited above, the effect of which is the 'excentration of the human essence' (Sève, 1974: 529).

The second thesis is:

The human essence does not have a human form, inasmuch as one understands by human form the form of a subject. Human social activity occurs in a patrimony of objects and relations which, from our point of view, is psychological action objectified in a non-psychological form, which becomes psychological activity again only when appropriated by individuals in the course of their development.

In the objective material form of this social patrimony there are not sentiments but regulations of activity, not conceptual thought but abstractions materialized. Thus the *essence* of human psychology is socially objectified while its psychic form remains inseparable from individuality, with its biological characteristics, and exists only in individuals. (pp. 529–30)

The third thesis is:

The psychology of personality is in a position radically second to the science of social relations without which it cannot exist. (p. 352)

These three theses spell out what Seve calls the Copernican revolution of Marxist social theory. 'Personality is the scientific concept which responds to two simple formulae: that which a man makes of his life; that which his life makes of him' (p. 538). What is required, then, is a 'science of biography equivalent in depth to the science of history founded by Marx and Engels, biography being to the personality what history is to society' (p. 538).

The biographical concept of personality — as the individual form of social relations — leads to the view that 'personality is not architecture notwithstanding that which underlies most existing theories of personality...it is a system of processes organized in time' (p. 345). One may add that this is also the view of radical behaviourism. For that matter, it is the view taken in constructing all information processing models.

How is individuality achieved? 'The social division of work, with all its consequences, is the social base of human individuation; and this follows from the excentration of human essence' (p. 346). Sève wishes to avoid the conclusion that there are uniform types of persons corresponding to occupations — this would confound 'the social matrices of activity and concrete psychological forms', and for this he relies on the factors of chance, liberty, and biological differences (p. 347).

He remarks that one sees

the nature of the frontier between psychosociology and the psychology of personality as it is conceived of here. This frontier rests entirely on the fundamental distinction between individuality and the individual, in other words on the excentration of human essence, which is the non-psychological nature of the forms of individuality, totally misunderstood by speculative humanism and the ordinary psychological ideology of which it is the basis; and its psychological form in the concrete individual. (p. 348)

Pursuing a rather tortuous path, Sève remarks further:

It is essential not to confuse the general social bases of the individual, in other words, the theory of individuality, which does not belong to the psychology of personality, and the most general aspect of the theory of the individual, the temporal topology of the personality, which is its heart. (p. 348)

These remarks are interesting, but they do not add up to a psychology. If we compare them with the approach of radical behaviourism, we see many similarities, with the difference that the focus of radical behaviourism on the individual case has led to more definite conceptions of the shaping of individual differences by environments with different logics. In radical behaviourism, the unit of behaviour is a triple consisting of a discriminative stimulus, an operant, and a reinforcing stimulus. The logic of the arrangement is called a contingency. We can easily see how individuation occurs in different environments with different logics. Where there are very few contingencies available, individuals will resemble each other very closely in their behaviour. Where there are many contingencies available, individuals may differ rather considerably, and much will depend on the chain of contingencies which they follow. The concept of *chance* simply refers to those variations which are not the object of the experiment. The concept of *objective liberty* refers to the chains of the environments open to the individual, and to the rigour of the contingencies which operate in these environments. The concept of subjective liberty will refer to sentiment, the private experience of constraint or freedom, which the individual is aware of in various environments. According to this view, psychology consists of the careful study of the most effective contingencies for shaping behaviour. This means that there is careful evaluation of reinforcers, stimulus conditions, the total logic of the environment (the schedule of reinforcement), and the repertoire of behaviour which the animal possesses.

The distinction between the logic of the environment (or the relations of production) and the shaping of the individual by this logic is quite clear. Sociology, one might say, would study environments and psychology would study the shaping of the individual in these environments. If we wished to create the greatest possible objective freedom, we would arrange for individuals to move freely along chains of environment towards whatever goals they desired. Unfortunately, these desires are produced in prior environments, so one would have to resort to some other criterion of freedom to create desires which could be satisfied.

Sève is clearly not content with sociologism as an account of the constitution of persons, who have to 'appropriate' the relation they observe, but he has very little to say about the nature of this appropriation.

We need to say something more here.

A conversational view

The conversational view of the relation between individual persons and the society they live in depends upon the following observations:

We can engage in conversation with others and are influenced but not always controlled by what they say. This means that our behaviour is intelligible rather than predictable.

We are able to represent what we do and act on these representations.

Each person has a number of identities and, therefore, a number of perspectives on a problem. This makes internal conversation possible and even profitable. Once more, the consequence is intelligibility rather than predictability.

We do not have to understand ourselves by our own unaided efforts. Knowledge can be codified and exchanged.

The conversational view asserts that the acts of persons may be intelligible if we know the context of these acts, but that they cannot be said to be determined by this context. This is because these acts exist in the realm of meaning and significance: the relations between them can be described in terms of aesthetics, logic, implication, metaphor, or dramatic intention. This is not to assert that they exist outside the realm of matter, or that they are not performed by material agents, but that matter, when it is organized in certain ways, is capable of actions which cannot be reduced to the language of cause-and-effect without losing their significance.

To understand this, we need to consider immediately the next property of persons. They can represent both themselves and their actions – and others and their actions – and these representations influence behaviour. We do not assert that this representation is complete (no representational system can include in its representation that representation of itself, for one thing), but it has important consequences. Because persons can represent their relations with others – including any prediction others may make about their behaviour – they are essentially unpredictable, as D. M. Mackay (1970) points out.

These self-representations are not the independent work of any isolated individual. Each person has at her disposal the work of many others in the form of gossip, art and theory, to assist or confuse her in her search for understanding.

Another way of saying some of what has been said, is to refer to the property of duality in our language and activity. Every message has a meta-message; every activity can be monitored as a performance, embodied in some frame of meaning. This property means that we can make the frame of an activity the focus of attention in a new activity. We can focus on an ideology, or on the nature of ideologies. The fact that we are not only information-processing animals but can become aware of our information-processing is crucial in a conversational model of the development of persons and identity. What we do is often invisible to us, but we can, more or less deliberately, become aware of how we are doing it and why we are doing it. We may do so by training (rhetoric, dramatic art, philosophy, mathematics, psychotherapy) to increase our knowledge of objects and our knowledge of personal processes, such as values, motives, mannerisms, behaviour (Boxer, 1979).

Awareness is not in itself enough to explain significant action. It may start unease and a search, though, in which we use prototypes of past activity (Bregman, 1977). These are transformed by changing proportions, changing context, exaggerating certain features, focusing on parts to discover the hidden figures we need, reversals or simple changes of scope.

An important source of knowledge is the conversations a woman has with herself as well as the conversations she has with others. Women can converse with themselves because the self has a variety of 'moments' or identifications. There is 'being-for-self' and 'being-for-others' (Hegel, 1929). In Mead's words, the 'I' is the response of the organism to the attitudes of others; the 'me' is the organized set of attitudes of others which a person assumes (Mead, 1934). Mead and Hegel are dividing up the problem in slightly different ways, but both are pointing to the fact that the self has different forms, even where it is at its most coherent. But in fact, the self has great difficulty in remaining coherent. The conversation, set up in early childhood, continues to supply problems and lead to solutions. When I grasp some aspect of the self as a datum, attempting to construe it, who joins the conversation? There is my ideal self, my self as I am, my self as I appear to John Smith, my self as I appear to my boss, my self as I was, and my self as I will be if I fail this examination. Not only this, but there are some of the selves of others in the space of the conversation we are having: John appears to like me, but is that his 'real self'?

These 'selves' or 'moments of self' are grouped in their most socially organized form as identities: the fact that a woman has different identities (she is a mother, a concert pianist, and a supporter of the Liberal Party) means that she can converse with herself in an interesting and informed way. She does not take one aspect of herself to be the whole. She can quarrel with what she is doing. Sometimes, as we know, the task of reconciling her different identities is so great that she becomes confused and wonders who she is. This is worst when none of these identities seems to be of any value; when they are all interesting she is more likely to be very busy than to be worried about who she is.

In its pathological form, there may be a dissociation of self and its corresponding identities (Osgood, Luria, Jeans and Smith, 1976).

In its normal form, the conversation a woman conducts with herself means that she cannot be reduced to that ideological mask which we described as a persona. Because she questions her beliefs, often rather sharply, she is often led to a critical examination of her personal ideology (and certainly the ruling ideology!).

In this internal conversation, she will certainly take hints from what others have done: she will know the questions and some of the answers of Marxists, Buddhists, Christians, existentialists, stoics, hedonists and so forth.

She does this because she knows very well that the quality of the ideology she uses in construing herself and others will make a difference to the quality of her achievements, in exactly the way that the quality of the instruments she uses in music or making clothes will make a difference to the quality of her work. If she construes herself as a mechanical and limited object, she will have mechanical and limited relations with herself and others.

She should (and she can) invent and use the best ideologies in the way she composes new music and uses the best techniques in playing Scarlatti. There is no recipe for the invention of new ideologies (or for the invention of anything else) but she will know when she has succeeded. She will find that she is more authentic in her relations with herself and others and that the world seems a more interesting place to her than it did. She knows that what is needed is an experimental approach to the development of tools and practices (in schools, in mental hospitals, in families). Many such experimental groups exist, attempting to gain everything from better working conditions to political and social revolution. She knows that they should be judged by their dogmatism, by their attitude to revision. Do they profess to be the whole truth? If so, she rejects them.

She knows how strong the fanatics are and how attractive their position is to many, especially in troubled countries like South Africa, Cambodia, Vietnam, Iran and even (strangely enough) the prosperous countries of Western Europe. The attraction of fanaticism is that one can stop criticizing oneself and start criticizing others, which is much more amusing. One can stop being so uncertain. How one longs for the suicide of reason sometimes!

But, because she has many responsibilities and does not shirk them, and because she is not a mechanism but a human being, she resists fanaticism and the slavery of dogmatic ideology. She will not simply 'reflect' what others call her position in society. She knows that women have been kept in their places for too long by such means.

Therefore, she believes in conversation. She will use violence only to protect herself from violence; and certainly she will not do herself the violence of ending the conversations by which she goes beyond the ideologies other people provide.

And how can social scientists help her? Why, by offering her something interesting to think about. And by making social science into a science of ideology and not simply one more ideology among others.

References

Althusser, L. and Balibar, E., 1975. *Lire le capital I.* Paris: Maspéro.
Asch, S. E., 1956. Studies of independence and conformity: a minority of one against a unanimous majority. *Psychological Monographs*, 70, Whole number 416.
Austin, J. L., 1962. *How to do things with words.* Oxford: Oxford University Press.
Bannister, D., and Fransella, Fay, 1971. *Inquiring man.* Harmondsworth: Penguin.
Bateson, G., Jackson, D. D., Haley, J., and Weakland, J., 1956. Toward a theory of schizophrenia. *Behavioural Science*, 1, 251–64.
Baumann, B., 1969. George H. Mead and Luigi Pirandello: Some parallels between the theoretical and artistic presentation of the social role concept. In P. Berger (ed.), *Marxism and sociology: views from Eastern Europe.* New York: Appleton-Century-Crofts.
Benveniste, E., 1966. *Problèmes de linguistiques générale.* Paris: Gallimard.
Berne, E., 1967. *Games people play.* Harmondsworth: Penguin.
Bernstein, B. B., 1961. Social structure, language and learning. *Educational Research*, 3, 163–76.

Bourdieu P. and Passeron, J. D. 1970. *La reproduction.* Paris: Editions de Minuit.
Boxer, P., 1979. Supporting reflective learning. Paper presented at the third International Congress on Personal Construct Psychology, Nijenrode.
Breakwell, G., 1978. Some effects of marginal social identity. In H. Tajfel (ed.), *Differentiation between social groups.* London: Academic Press.
Bregman, A. S., 1977. Perception and behavior as compositions of ideals. *Cognitive Psychology,* 9, 250–92.
Brown, Roger, 1965. *Social psychology.* Glencoe Ill.: Free Press.
Brown, Roger and Herrnstein, R. J., 1975. *Psychology.* London: Methuen.
Brown, Rupert, 1978. Divided we fall: an analysis of relations between sections of a factory workforce. In H. Tajfel (ed.), *Differentiation between social groups.* London: Academic Press.
Cot, J. -P. and Mounière, J. -P., 1974. *Pour une sociologie politique.* Paris: Seuil.
Dahrendorf, R., 1959. *Class and class conflict in industrial society.* London: Routledge.
De Klerk, W., 1975. *The puritans in Africa.* London: Rex Collings.
Desmond, C. [n. d.]. *The discarded people.* Johannesburg: The Christian Institute of South Africa.
Devereux, G., 1975. Ethnic identity: its logical foundations and its dysfunctions. In G. de Vos and L. Romanucci-Ross (eds), *Ethnic identity: cultural continuities and change.* Palo Alto: Mayfield.
Doise, W., Deschamps, J. C., and Meyer, C., 1978. The accentuation of intra-group similarities. In H. Tajfel (ed.), *Differentiation between social groups.* London: Academic Press.
Edelman, M., 1971. *Politics as symbolic action: mass arousal and quiescence.* New York: Academic Press.

Ellis, G. F. R., 1974. On understanding the world and the universe. Inaugural lecture, University of Cape Town.

Erikson, E., 1968. *Identity.* London: Faber.

Fanon, F., 1970. *Black skin white masks.* London: Paladin.

Fodor, J. A., 1968. *Psychological explanation.* New York: Random House.

Freire, P., 1972. *Pedagogy of the oppressed.* Harmondsworth: Penguin.

Garfinkel, H., 1967. *Studies in ethnomethodology.* Englewood Cliffs, New Jersey: Prentice-Hall.

Gerth, H., and Mills, C. W., 1954. *Character and social structure.* London: Routledge.

Giles, H., Bourhis, R. Y., and Taylor, D. M., 1979. Towards a theory of language in ethnic group relations. In H. Giles (ed.), *Language, ethnicity and intergroup relations.* London: Academic Press.

Goffman, E., 1968. *Stigma: notes on the management of spoiled identity.* Harmondsworth: Penguin.

Goffman, E., 1969. *The presentation of self in everyday life.* London: Allen Lane, The Penguin Press.

Goffman, E., 1975. *Frame analysis.* Harmondsworth: Penguin.

Harré, R., 1979. *Social being.* Oxford: Blackwell.

Harré, R., and Secord, P. F., 1972. *The explanation of social behaviour.* Oxford: Blackwell.

Hayek, F. A., 1978. The miscarriage of the democratic ideal. *Encounter,* 50, 14–17.

Hegel, G., 1929. *Science of logic.* London: Muirhead Library of Philosophy.

Illich, I., 1973. *Deschooling society.* Harmondsworth: Penguin.

Jakobson, R., 1963. *Essais de linguistique générale.* Paris: Editions de Minuit.

James, H., 1968. *Selected literary criticism.* Harmondsworth: Penguin.

Jaworskyj, M. (ed.), 1967. *Soviet political thought.* Baltimore:

The Johns Hopkins Press.
Johnstone, F., 1976. *Class, race and gold.* London: Routledge.
Jung, C. G., 1959. *Collected works*, vol 9. London: Routledge.
Kelly, G. A., 1955. *The psychology of personal constructs (2) vols).* New York: Norton.
Kelly, G. A., 1962. Europe's matrix of decision. In M. R. Jones (ed.), *Nebraska Symposium of Motivation.* Lincoln: Nebraska University Press.
Kelly, G. A., 1963. *A theory of personality.* New York: Norton.
Koch, S., 1954. Clark L. Hull. In W. Estes (ed.), *Modern learning theory.* New York: Appleton-Century-Crofts.
Kuhn, T. S., 1962, rev. ed. 1970. *The structure of scientific revolutions.* Chicago: University of Chicago Press.
Lacan, J., 1966. *Ecrits.* Paris: Seuil.
Laing, R. D., 1962. Series and nexus in the family. *New Left Review,* 15, 7–14.
Lem, S., 1979. No nonsense. *Encounter,* 52, 3–7.
Lemaine, G., Kastersztein, J. and Personnaz, B., 1978. Social differentiation. In Tajfel, H. (ed.), *Differentiation between social groups.* London: Academic Press.
MacIntyre, A., 1971. *Against the self-images of the age.* New York: Schocken Books.
Mackay, D. M., 1970. *Information, mechanism and meaning.* Cambridge, Mass.: M.I.T. Press.
Mackay, N., 1975. Psychological explanation. Unpublished M.Sc. thesis, University of Cape Town.
McKellar, P., 1977. The Jekyll and Hyde in all of us. *Psychology Today* (1977), 44–6.
Mair, J. M. M., 1977. Community of selves. In D. Bannister (ed.), *New perspectives in personal construct theory.* London: Academic Press.
Malraux, A., 1970. *Antimemoirs.* Harmondsworth: Penguin.
Mannheim, K., 1936. *Ideology and utopia.* London: Kegan Paul.

Mannoni, O., 1956. *Prospero and Caliban: the psychology of colonization.* London: Methuen.
Marx, K., 1973. *Surveys from exile.* Harmondsworth: Penguin.
Mead, G. H., 1934. *Mind, self and society.* Chicago: University of Chicago Press.
Milgram, S., 1974. *Obedience to authority.* London: Tavistock.
Mills, C. W., 1963. *The Marxists.* Harmondsworth: Penguin.
Moles, A., 1968. *Information theory and esthetic perception.* Urbana: University of Illinois Press.
Moscovici, S., and Paichler, G., 1978. Social comparison and social recognition: two complementary processes of identification. In H. Tajfel (ed.), *Differentiation between social groups.* London: Academic Press.
Mulder, C. P., and Cruywagen, W. A. (eds), 1968. *1948–1968 ...en nou die toekoms! A survey of the achievements of the national party government from 1948–1968.* Johannesburg: Voortrekkerpers.
Osgood, C. E., Luria, Z., Jeans, R. F., and Smith, S. W., 1976. The three faces of Evelyn: a case report. *Journal of Abnormal Psychology*, 85, 247–86.
Phillips, D. L., 1977. *Wittgenstein and scientific knowledge.* London: Macmillan.
Popper, K., 1966. *The open society and its enemies.* London: Routledge and Kegan Paul.
Renard, M., 1975. Review: Les masques d'un homme sans nom. *Le Monde*, August.
Robbe-Grillet, A., 1963. *Pour un nouveau roman.* Paris: Editions de minuit.
Ross, L., Amabile, T., and Steinmetz, J., 1977. Social roles, social control, and biases in social-perception processes. *Journal of Personality and Social Psychology*, 35, 485–94.
Russell, B., 1940. *An inquiry into meaning and truth.* London: Allen and Unwin.
Russell, B., 1961. *History of western philosophy.* London:

George Allen and Unwin.
Scott, B., and Lyman, S. M., 1972. Accounts. In J. G. Manis and B. N. Meltzer (eds), *Symbolic interaction.* Boston: Allyn and Bacon.
Searle, J. R., 1969. *Speech acts.* Cambridge: Cambridge University Press.
Sève, L., 1974. *Marxisme et théorie de la personnalité.* Paris: Editions Sociales.
Shaw, M. L. G., and McKnight, C., 1979. An exploration of intra-personal personalities. Paper presented at the third International Congress on Personal Construct Psychology, Nijenrode.
Sidney, P., 1922. An apology for poetry. In E. D. Jones (ed.), *English critical essays.* London: Oxford University Press.
Strachey, L., 1948. *Eminent Victorians.* Harmondsworth: Penguin.
Strawson, P. F., 1959. *Individuals: an essay in descriptive metaphysics.* London: Methuen.
Survey of Race Relations in South Africa 1977. Johannesburg: South African Institute of Race Relations, 1978.
Tajfel, H., 1972. La catégorisation sociale, In S. Moscovici (ed.), *Introduction à la psychologie sociale*, vol. 1. Paris: Larousse.
Tajfel, H. (ed.), 1978. *Differentiation between social groups.* London: Academic Press.
Tawney, R. H., 1938. *Religion and the rise of capitalism.* Harmondsworth: Penguin.
Tey, J., 1951. *The daughters of time.* Harmondsworth: Penguin.
Tobias, P. V., 1972. *The meaning of race.* Johannesburg: South African Institute of Race Relations.
Turner, J., 1975. Social comparison and social identity: some prospects for intergroup behaviour. *European Journal of Social Psychology*, 5, 5–34.
van Jaarsveld, F. A., 1961. *The awakening of Afrikaner nationalism.* Cape Town: Human and Rousseau.

Vaughan, G. M., 1978. Social change and intergroup preferences in New Zealand. *European Journal of Social Psychology*, 8, 297–314.

Veblen, T., 1899. *The theory of the leisure class.* New York: Macmillan.

Watzlawick, P., Beavin, J. H., and Jackson, D. D., 1968. *Pragmatics of human communication.* London: Faber.

Wilson, F., 1972. *Labour in the South African gold mines.* Cambridge: Cambridge University Press.

Wittgenstein, L., 1953. *Philosophical investigations.* New York: Macmillan.

Wittgenstein, L., 1967. *Remarks on the foundations of mathematics.* Cambridge, Mass.: M.I.T. Press.

Zimbardo, P. G., 1975. Transforming experimental research into advocacy for social change. In M. Deutsch and H. A. Hornstein (eds), *Applying social psychology.* Hillsdale: Lawrence Erlbaum Associates.

Name Index

Adams, A. 108
Africa, W. S. 107, 108
Althusser, L. 51
Amabile, T. 62
Asch, S. E. 68, 105
Austin, J. L. 16
Balibar, E. 51
Bannister, D. 121, 127
Bateson, G. 30
Baumann, B. 1, 9
Beavin, J. H. 30
Benveniste, E. 14
Bergins, W. J. 107
Berne, E. 30, 46
Bernstein, B. B. 61
Boezak, L. D. 109
Botha, M. C. 87, 142
Botha, P. W. 86, 118
Bourdieu, P. 62
Bourhis, R. 106
Boxer, P. 81, 162
Breakwell, G. 105
Bregman, A. S. 162
Brown, Roger 65, 115
Brown, Rupert 24
Coetzee, B. 89

Cot, J.-P. 63, 65
Cruywagen, W. A. 126
Curry, D. 108
Dahrendorf, R. 9, 23, 95
de Jager, P. R. 88
de Klerk, W. A. 116
Deschamps, J. C. 3
Desmond, C. 97
Devereux, G. 7, 27
Doise, W. 3
Ebrahim, C. H. 109
Edelman, M. 81, 111
Ellis, G. F. R. 97
Erikson, E. 6, 7, 76, 117
Fanon, F. 74
Fodor, J. A. 153
Fransella, F. 121, 127
Froneman, G. F. 86, 87, 88, 89, 97
Garfinkel, H. 113
Gerth, H. 27, 133, 146
Giles, H. 106
Goffman, E. 17, 20, 68
Grobler, M. S. F. 86, 89, 141
Haley, J. 30
Harré, R. 3, 12, 15, 113

NAME INDEX

Hayek, F. A. 9
Haywood, J. J. 87
Hegel, G. 162
Hernstein, R. 65
Hopkins, G. M. 31
Illich, I. 9
Jackson, D. D. 30
Jacobs, A. C. 109
Jakobson, R. 14
James, H. 33
Jansen, E. G. 88
Jaworskyj, M. 52
Jeans, R. F. 8, 163
Johnstone, F. 24
Jonker, A. 86
Jung, C. G. 76
Kastersztein, J. 18
Kelly, G. A. 9, 34, 35, 36, 111, 121–45 *passim*
Kipling, R. 75
Koch, S. 154
Kuhn, T. S. 55
Lacan, J. 32
Laing, R. D. 117
Lem, S. 21
Lemaine, G. 18
Leon, L. S. 109
Liebenberg, J. V. L. 85
Luria, Z. 8, 163
Luther, M. 38
Lyman, B. 6, 32
Mackay, D. M. 161
Mackay, N. 153
MacIntyre, A. 49
McKellar, P. 8
McKnight, C. 8
Mair, M. 8
Malan, D. 85, 101, 128, 129
Malraux, A. 110, 124

Mannheim, K. 51
Mannoni, O. 74
Marais, P. 126
Maree, W. A. 87
Martins, H. E. 86, 114
Marx, K. 43–52 *passim*, 152
Mead, G. H. 162
Meyer, G. 3
Milgram, S. 68, 105
Mills, C. W. 8, 27, 133, 146
Moles, A. 81
Moore, P. A. 114
Moscovici, S. 18
Mounière, J.-P. 63, 65
Mulder, C. P. 126
Muller, J. 108
Nash J. H. 109
Nel, M. D. C. 85, 87
Osgood, C. E. 8, 163
Paichler, G. 18
Passeron, J. D. 62
Personnaz, B. 18
Pienaar, B. 89
Phillips, D. L. 26, 55, 58
Popper, K. 25
Rabie, J. A. 109
Raubenheimer, A. L. 89
Reed, C. J. 109
Renard, M. 37
Robbe-Grillet, A. 20
Ross, L. 62
Roux, P. C. 89
Russell, B. 21, 53, 60
Sadie, N. C. 89
Schlegel, 4
Scholtz, D. J. 86
Scott, B. 6, 32
Searle, J. 120
Secord, P. 15, 113

Seve, L. 157–60 *passim*
Shaw, M. L. G. 8
Sidney, P. 79
Smith, S. W. 8, 163
Steinmetz, J. 62
Steyn, A. 86
Strachey, L. 63
Strawson, P. F. 78
Strydom, G. H. F. 86, 88, 115
Strydom, J. G. 86
Swartz, W. J. 107
Tajfel, H. 17, 21, 22, 40
Tawney, R. H. 118
Taylor, D. M. 106
Tey, J. 4
Tobias, P. V. 62

Turner, J. 21, 22
Van den Berg, M. J. 87, 90
Van Jaarsveld, F. A. 4
Van Niekerk, J. G. W. 85
Van Rhyn, A. J. R. 87, 119
Vaughan, G. M. 23
Veblen, T. 3
Verwoerd, H. 70, 88
Vorster, J. B. 88, 101, 102, 114, 126
Vosloo, A. 89
Watzlawick, P. 30
Weakland, J. 30
Wilson, F. 24, 98
Wittgenstein, L. 26, 56
Zimbardo, P. G. 68, 105

Subject Index

Aesthetic versus semantic content of messages, 81
Afrikaner, 92, 102, 114, 117
Agents, core constructs of, 123; differentiation of, 17; ecology, 18; individual and collective, 12–17
Behaviourism versus mentalism, 153
Conversational theory of ideology, 151, 160
Conversations, internal, 162
Categories, logical difficulties, 57
Categorizing and characterizing, 78
Centralization versus decentralization, 9
Character and incident, 33
Choice and image, 120
Class, and identity, 95; and power, 95; representatives of, 45; and schools, 62
Clear cases, 83, 134
Collectives, 12–17
Coloured Persons' Representative Council, 104–10
Competition and differentiation of agents, 19, 21–5
Constructs, choice, 127; commonality, 122; construct theory, 121; core, 123; dichotomy, 131; elaboration, 127; motive, 133; organization, 145
Control, 30
Dichotomy, 35, 131
Dictionary of constructs, 134–7
Differentials, 24–5
Differentiation of agents, competition, 19, 21–5; interaction, 20–1; open and closed ideology, 25–8
Distributive justice, 65
Ecology of agents, 18
Economic interests, 143
Educational theory, 66
Ego, 7, 117
Episode, 113, 116
Evaluation of identities, 96
Evolution of social structure versus revolution, 29, 40
Excentration of human essence, 157

SUBJECT INDEX 177

Expressive and practical order, 3, 12, 25
Family resemblances, 59, 67
Fractions, 44
Frame analysis, 67
Great Trek, 123
Historical materialism, 50–4
Identity, collective, 13; con, 73, 104; cuckoo, 76; dimensions, 90, 91; evaluation, 96; frame, 3, 67, 71, 100; and ideology, 5, 28; and interests, 1; negotiated, 19; new, 39; versus person, 7; pivotal or reference, 83; and politics, 3; problematic, 31; versus self, 7; structure, 90; traps, 6, 29, 30, 71, 76
Ideological apparatus, 61
Ideology, concept, 43; forms, 46; generality, 47; images, 111; and individual, 47; and material conditions, 50; and meaning, 44; as metaphor, 45; open and closed, 19, 25; and paradigm, 55; richness, 28, 41; and social structure, 53
Image, 111, 113; and limits of choice, 120
Incident, 112
Incommensurability, 57
Individuals, 46
Intelligentsia, 45
Interaction assumption, 19, 20
Knowledge, engagements, 59; incommensurability, 57; language games, 55; paradigms, 55; positivism, 55; relativization, 57
Language games, 26, 55
Liberalism, 49, 110

Liberty, 159
Logic and guides to action, 53
Logic of environment, 159
Marxism, critique, 51–4; view of ideology, 43–6; view of personality, 157
Masks, 44, 50
Material versus spiritual, 48
Material conditions and ideology, 44
Materialist conception of history, 51
Meaning versus information, 81
Messages, 81
Metaphor, and identity, 92; and ideology, 44
Methodology for identity frame, 83, 99
Modes of address, 115
Modes of thought and property, 44
Motives, 133
Mystification, 49
Open and closed ideology, 25–8
Paradigm, 55–8
Person versus identity, 6
Persona versus person, 4, 76
Philosophy of science, 55
Pivotal figure in identity frame, 83
Politics, 1
Political activists, 23, 74
Political alternatives in South Africa, 100–4, 127–31
Policy, Construal of in South African House of Assembly, black identity, 141; black welfare, 143; conflict, 142; economic interests, 143; ethics, 145;

SUBJECT INDEX

index of depth of argument, 149; white identity and survival, 140
Poor law, 117
Positivism, 55
Pressure to change, 39
Puritanism, 117
Realism and ideology, 70
Reference identity, 83, 92
Reflection theory of ideology, 51, 151
Religion and politics, 68
Restricted code, 61
Revolutionary change, 29, 40
Role power, 62
Role versus identity, 5
Rugby, 63
School feeding, 116
Schooling versus personal learning, 9
Schools, and class, 62; and factory society, 66; and ideology, 62–7
Self, 7, 34; and anti-self, 35; appearances of, 162; and other, 36
Situation, 111
Social interaction and differentiation of agents, 19–21
Sociologism, 152
Solipsism, collective and individual, 10, 58
Sparta and Athens, 27
Squeeze, 71
Structure of identities, 90
Symbolic force, 65
Trekker, 94
Unemployment, black, 144
Ways of life, 48
Welfare, 143
White identity, 138
World views, 46, 68, 79